Eco-Catastrophe

by the Editors of Ramparts

HARPER & ROW, PUBLISHERS

NEW YORK, EVANSTON, AND LONDON

1817

About the cover:

Color photograph by Elihu Blotnick of People's
    Park

Black and white photograph by Richard Conrat
    of San Francisco Bay across from Phillips
    Oil Refinery

Copyright© 1970 by the Editors of Ramparts

LIBRARY OF CONGRESS CATALOG CARD NUMBER: 70-115464

Forward

Among the hundreds of books on ecology and the environment that have already appeared in print, *Eco-Catastrophe!* is undoubtedly unique. For the writers in this volume do not see the ecology crisis as merely one among a number of distinct social problems, which bear only a superficial relation to one another. On the contrary, the destruction of the living environment is seen to be an integral part of the general social crisis in America: the oppression of minority peoples, the genocidal war against the Vietnamese, and the accelerating repression of all militant forces for social progress and change. Like the race crisis and the Vietnam War, the ecological impasse is not merely the result of bad or mistaken policies that can be changed by a new Administration or a new will to do better. It is, rather, the expression of a basic malfunction of the social order itself, and consequently cannot be dealt with on a piecemeal, patchwork basis. In short, this volume of articles, originally appearing in *Ramparts* articulates a *radical* perspective, locating the root of the ecological crisis in the very structure of American society, and pointing to the necessity of a revolutionary reconstruction of that social order as a precondition for any practical and effective reform. That this recognition should be the source of *Eco-Catastrophe*'s uniqueness among books on ecology only indicates further the magnitude of that crisis and the distance that separates us from any viable solution.

David Horowitz

Editorial

The environment may well be the gut issue that can unify a polarized nation in the 1970's, writes Time magazine. The Hearst Press sees it as a movement "that could unite the generations." And the New York Times solemnly predicts that ecology "will replace Vietnam as the major issue with students."

The wishful thinking of a frightened Establishment? Perhaps. But the organizers of the officially-sanctioned April 22 Teach-In movement are doing their best to give life to the media's daydream about the co-optive potential of ecology. If they succeed, thousands of young people across the country will engage in a series of environmental extravaganzas, embellished to capture the excitement of the original Vietnam teach-ins, but structured to encourage the young to forsake the "less important issues" and enlist in a crusade to save the earth.

We think that any analogy between what is supposed to happen around April 22 and the organization of the Vietnam teach-ins is obscene. We think that the Environmental Teach-In apparatus is the first step in a con game that will do little more than abuse the environment even further. We do not think it will succeed.

The originators of the Vietnam teach-ins worked at great odds and against the lies and opposition of government, university administrations and the media. They raised their own money and had offices in student apartments or small storefronts. "Earth Day" came to life in the offices of Senator Gaylord Nelson, received blessings from Nixon's Department of Health, Education and Welfare, was funded by foundations, and has worked out of facilities lent by the Urban Coalition.

Vietnam protestors had to create their own reading lists, fact sheets and white papers; they had to work against the "expertise" of Southeast Asia scholars. The Environmental Teach-In comes pre-packaged; a well-paid and well-staffed national office sends local organizers an official brochure which avoids mentioning the social and economic environment with which Mother Nature has to cope.

Friends of the Earth (FOE) provides, through Ballantine Books, a semi-official "Environmental Handbook," which insists that saving the environment "transcends the other issues" and that we should in non-partisan fashion "support a man from any political party if he is a true Friend of the Earth."

Never mind if he's a racist. Don't worry about whether or not he supports American imperialism. This spring the Nixon Administration is busy undoing 15 years of struggle for school integration; the police continue to murder black people in the streets; the American judicial system is disintegrating and, in the eyes of the State, every radical has become a conspirator; the war machine in Washington has made clear its intention to stay in Vietnam indefinitely and to spread its war to Laos. All this—and the Teach-In organizers want to banish everything but environment to the back pages of our minds. They must be blind, or perverse, or both.

How can anyone in this dark springtime believe kind words—about environment or anything else—from the men in power? Once we might have been able to believe that because a President had embraced the civil rights issue, apartheid in the Deep South was dead. But such illusions can hardly be sustained any longer. The Open Housing Act, the chief legislative victory of those years, finds use this season only for its "H. Rap Brown Amendment"—the interstate travel ban on which the Justice Department hung the Chicago 7.

Lyndon Johnson promised that We Shall Overcome. Now Richard Nixon promises to clean up America. Even TV's "Laugh-In" knows the punch-line: "If Nixon's War on Pollution is as successful as Johnson's War on Poverty, we're going to have an awful lot of dirty poor people around."

Haven't we learned after a decade of social struggle that major problems like Vietnam, Race, Poverty—now Environment—can't be packaged separately, each protected from contamination by "other issues"? Even the Kerner Commission realized that white racism was systematic, structural and linked to economic and social institutions. Even the most determined skeptic has now been shown by the Nixon Administration that the Vietnam war was no honest mistake, but the result of a long history of American expansion into Asia and a long-term policy of subjecting poor nations to the imperatives of American investors. To understand why Washington has persisted in its genocidal war in Indo-China, don't look at the politicians who come and go; look at the structures of power and interest that remain.

[II]

Threats to the environment are no different. At their source is the same division of society—those with power against those without: the corporations, which organize for their own benefit, against the people whom they organize destructively.

Look at the values which galvanize energies and allocate resources in the business system: pursuit of money, enrichment of self, the exploitation of man—and of nature—to generate still more money. Is it surprising that a system seeking to turn everything into gold ends up turning everything into garbage? The market is master. Business makes money meeting consumer demands; it makes even more money creating new demands. More money is spent on advertising and sales promotion in America, on planned obsolescence and consumer manipulation, than on all education—public and private, elementary school through the university. This is pollution of the mind, and it has its own costs. Some students estimate that socially useless, ecologically disastrous waste products make up nearly half of the Gross National Product. Nixon has already predicted a 50 per cent increase in the GNP by 1980, ostensibly to finance new priorities like environmental reform. It would be better if he had questioned how much waste the dynamic American economy will have to produce in the next decade simply to clean up the waste of past decades.

Others, like the organizers of the National Teach-In, tell us that it is in the interest even of the corporate rich to clean up the environment. If all their customers are asphyxiated by air pollution, explain these optimists, business (and businessmen) would expire as well. By this same logic, the military-industrial complex should bar the ABM from its cities, and the corporations, always eager to bring new consumers into the market, should make the war on poverty work. But no businessman, alone or with other businessmen, can change the tendencies of this ultimately ecocidal process unless he puts the system out of business. As long as society organizes production around the incentive to convert man's energies and nature's resources into profit, no planned, equable, ecologically balanced system of production can ever exist. Teach-ins which fail to confront this fact of life do worse than teach nothing. They obstruct knowledge and stand in the way of a solution. They join the struggle on the side which permits them truly to say—not of mankind, but of themselves—"We have found the enemy and he is us."

Perhaps the Teach-Ins could teach better if, instead of their present brochure, they distributed a full-page ad from Fortune's special environment issue. Sponsored by the New York State Department of Commerce, the ad pictures Governor Nelson Rockefeller inviting businessmen to come grow with New York. The pitch is simple: "Personal property of manufacturers is completely exempt from taxation in New York . . . During the past eleven years, there has not been one single new business tax in New York." Nowhere does the ad mention New York's long series of new *nonbusiness* taxes. In 11 years in office, Rocky has first imposed, then hiked a new state sales tax; quadrupled the cigarette tax; tripled the gasoline tax; and lowered the minimum income below which poor people are free of the state income tax. Businesses apparently aren't expected to care who subsidizes their growth. But the ad does want them to know that Governor Rockefeller, author of the "soak-the-poor program," considers "economic growth—a continuing expansion of the private economy—to be the indispensable ingredient of all progress."

Rockefeller doesn't say this only because he's a Rockefeller; he says it because he's Governor and every governor wants business to invest in his state. Private business accounts for 85 per cent of the GNP; it must be kept happy and expanding, or, short of revolution, there will be nothing for anyone at all. Regulation of business consequently can never be more than self-regulation, federal intervention into the business sector never more than federal intervention on behalf of the business sector.

But regulation is not the question. We simply don't need any more gross national product, any more unnecessary goods and factories. What we do need is a *redistribution* of existing real wealth, and a *reallocation* of society's resources. Everyone knows what this redistribution and reallocation should do; the crises of the last ten years have made it all so obvious: The poor must have adequate income, the cities must be rebuilt to fit human requirements, the environment must be de-polluted, the educational system must be vastly expanded, and social energies now poured into meaningless pursuits (like advertising and sales promotion) must be rechanneled into humanly edifying and creative activities.

We must, in short, junk the business system and its way of life, and create revolutionary new institutions to embody new goals— human and environmental.

All this sounds utopian. Well, utopias are relative. More utopian by far than revolution is the idea that the present society, dominated by business, can create lasting, meaningful reforms sufficient, for example, to permit mankind to survive the century.

[III]

At a recent "Survival Faire" in San Jose, California, ecology organizers bought a new car and buried it as a symbol of the task which they saw confronting ecology action groups. This was an indication of dangerous political naivete that must be overcome. To buy the car in the first place was to pay the criminal and strengthen him. But this act also pointed the finger of guilt at the consumer, who has only the choice of traveling to work by auto or walking 30 miles to work on the freeway. In opposition to this misdirected gesture of revolt, San Jose's black students angrily demanded that the car be raffled to provide defense funds for their brothers on trial. The blacks made their point very clearly. "Don't bury the car," their placard said, "bury the system."

In contrast to this Survival Faire, the week after the Conspiracy defendants were sentenced in Chicago, angry students razed the local branch of the Bank of America in Santa Barbara, California. The only bank in the Isla Vista youth ghetto, B of A had long treated young people as a class apart. It had opposed the grape strikers centered in Delano. It had supported, with branches in Saigon and Bangkok and with its leadership of the investment build-up in the Pacific, the American occupation of Southeast Asia. Two of its directors sit on the board of Union Oil, which had for so many months desecrated the once-beautiful beaches of Santa Barbara and destroyed their wildlife. Most important, as the branch manager explained to the press, it had been the major local symbol of capitalism and the business system.

Burning a bank is not the same as putting the banks and their system out of business. To do that, millions of people in this country will first have to wake up to the real source of their misery. The action in Santa Barbara, a community which has seen its environment destroyed by corporate greed, might spark that awakening. If it does, the students who burned the Bank of America in Santa Barbara will have done more to save the environment than all the Survival Faires and "Earth Day Teach-Ins" put together.

Editors of Ramparts

Contents

Eco-Catastrophe!

Dr. Paul Ehrlich

Wood Engraving by M.C. Escher

In the following scenario, Dr. Paul Ehrlich predicts what our world will be like in ten years if the present course of environmental destruction is allowed to continue. Dr. Ehrlich is a prominent ecologist, a professor of biology at Stanford University, and author of The Population Bomb *(Ballantine).*

[I]

The end of the ocean came late in the summer of 1979, and it came even more rapidly than the biologists had expected. There had been signs for more than a decade, commencing with the discovery in 1968 that DDT slows down photosynthesis in marine plant life. It was announced in a short paper in the technical journal, Science, but to ecologists it smacked of doomsday. They knew that all life in the sea depends on photosynthesis, the chemical process by which green plants bind the sun's energy and make it available to living things. And they knew that DDT and similar chlorinated hydrocarbons had polluted the entire surface of the earth, including the sea.

But that was only the first of many signs. There had been the final gasp of the whaling industry in 1973, and the end of the Peruvian anchovy fishery in 1975. Indeed, a score of other fisheries had disappeared quietly from over-exploitation and various eco-catastrophes by 1977. The term "eco-catastrophe" was coined by a California ecologist in 1969 to describe the most spectacular of man's attacks on the systems which sustain his life. He drew his inspiration from the Santa Barbara offshore oil disaster of that year, and from the news which spread among naturalists that virtually all of the Golden State's seashore bird life was doomed because of chlorinated hydrocarbon interference with its reproduction. Eco-catastrophes in the sea became increasingly common in the early 1970's. Mysterious "blooms" of previously rare micro-organisms began to appear in offshore waters. Red tides—killer outbreaks of a minute single-celled plant—returned to the Florida Gulf coast and were sometimes accompanied by tides of other exotic hues.

It was clear by 1975 that the entire ecology of the ocean was changing. A few types of phytoplankton were becoming resistant to chlorinated hydrocarbons and were gaining the upper hand. Changes in the phytoplankton community led inevitably to changes in the community of zooplankton, the tiny animals which eat the phytoplankton. These changes were passed on up the chains of life in the ocean to the herring, plaice, cod and tuna. As the diversity of life in the ocean diminished, its stability also decreased.

Other changes had taken place by 1975. Most ocean fishes that returned to fresh water to breed, like the salmon, had become extinct, their breeding streams so dammed up and polluted that their powerful homing instinct only resulted in suicide. Many fishes and shellfishes that bred in restricted areas along the coasts followed them as onshore pollution escalated.

By 1977 the annual yield of fish from the sea was down to 30 million metric tons, less than one-half the per capita catch of a decade earlier. This helped malnutrition to escalate sharply in a world where an estimated 50 million people per year were already dying of starvation. The United Nations attempted to get all chlorinated hydrocarbon insecticides banned on a worldwide basis, but the move was defeated by the United States. This opposition was generated primarily by the American petrochemical industry, operating hand in glove with its subsidiary, the United States Department of Agriculture. Together they persuaded the government to oppose the U.N. move—which was not difficult since most Americans believed that Russia and China were more in need of fish products than was the United States. The United Nations also attempted to get fishing nations to adopt strict and enforced catch limits to preserve dwindling stocks. This move was blocked by Russia, who, with the most modern electronic equipment, was in the best position to glean what was left in the sea. It was, curiously, on the very day in 1977 when the Soviet Union announced its refusal that another ominous article appeared in Science. It announced that incident solar radiation had been so reduced by worldwide air pollution that serious effects on the world's vegetation could be expected.

[II]

Apparently it was a combination of ecosystem destablization, sunlight reduction, and a rapid escalation in chlorinated hydrocarbon pollution from massive Thanodrin applications which triggered the ultimate catastrophe. Seventeen huge Soviet-financed Thanodrin plants were operating in underdeveloped countries by 1978. They had been part of a massive Russian "aid offensive" designed to fill the gap caused by the collapse of America's ballyhooed "Green Revolution."

It became apparent in the early '70s that the "Green Revolution" was more talk than substance. Distribution of high yield "miracle" grain seeds had caused temporary local spurts in agricultural production. Simultaneously, excellent weather had produced record harvests. The combintion permitted bureaucrats, especially in the United States Department of Agriculture and the Agency for International Development (AID), to reverse their previous pessimism and indulge in an outburst of optimistic propaganda about staving off famine. They raved about the approaching transformation of agriculture in the underdeveloped countries (UDCs). The reason for the propaganda reversal was never made clear. Most historians agree that a combination of utter ignorance of ecology, a desire to justify past errors, and pressure from agro-industry (which was eager to sell pesticides, fertilizers, and farm machinery to the UDCs and agencies helping the UDCs) was behind the campaign. Whatever the motivation, the results were clear. Many concerned people, lacking the expertise to see through the Green Revolution drivel, relaxed. The population-food crisis was "solved."

But reality was not long in showing itself. Local famine persisted in northern India even after good weather brought an end to the ghastly Bihar famine of the mid-'60s. East Pakistan was next, followed by a resurgence of general famine in northern India. Other foci of famine rapidly developed in Indonesia, the Philippines, Malawi, the Congo, Egypt, Colombia, Ecuador, Honduras, the Dominican Republic, and Mexico.

Everywhere hard realities destroyed the illusion of the Green Revolution. Yields dropped as the progressive farmers who had first accepted the new seeds found that their higher yields brought lower prices—effective demand (hunger plus cash) was not sufficient in poor countries to keep prices up. Less progressive farmers, observing this, refused to make the extra effort required to cultivate the "miracle" grains. Transport systems proved inadequate to bring the necessary fertilizer to the fields where the new and extremely fertilizer-sensitive grains were being grown. The same systems were also inadequate to move produce to markets. Fertilizer plants were not built fast enough, and most of the underdeveloped countries could not scrape together funds to purchase supplies, even on concessional terms. Finally, the inevitable happened, and pests began to reduce yields in even the most carefully cultivated fields. Among the first were the famous "miracle rats" which invaded Philippine "miracle rice" fields early in 1969. They were quickly followed by many insects and viruses, thriving on the relatively pest-susceptible new grains, encouraged by the vast and dense plantings, and rapidly acquiring resistance to the chemicals used against them. As chaos spread until even the most obtuse agriculturists and economists realized that the Green Revolution had turned brown, the Russians stepped in.

In retrospect it seems incredible that the Russians, with the American mistakes known to them, could launch an even more incompetent program of aid to the underdeveloped world. Indeed, in the early 1970's there were cynics in the United States who claimed that outdoing the stupidity of American foreign aid would be physically impossible. Those critics were, however, obviously unaware that the Russians had been busily destroying their own environment for many years. The virtual disappearance of sturgeon from Russian rivers caused a great shortage of caviar by 1970. A standard joke among Russian scientists at that time was that they had created an artificial caviar which was indistinguishable from the real thing—except by taste. At any rate the Soviet Union, observing with interest the progressive deterioration of relations between the UDCs and the United States, came up with a solution. It had recently developed what it claimed was the ideal insecticide, a highly lethal chlorinated hydrocarbon complexed with a special agent for penetrating the external skeletal armor of insects. Announcing that the new pesticide, called Thanodrin, would truly produce a Green Revolution, the Soviets entered into negotiations with various UDCs for the construction of massive Thanodrin factories. The USSR would bear all the costs; all it wanted in return were certain trade and military concessions.

It is interesting now, with the perspective of years, to examine in some detail the reasons why the UDCs welcomed the Thanodrin plan with such open arms. Government officials in these countries ignored the protests of their own scientists that Thanodrin would not solve the problems which plagued them. The governments now knew that the basic cause of their problems was overpopulation, and that these problems had been exacerbated by the dullness, daydreaming, and cupidity endemic to all governments. They knew that only population control and limited development aimed primarily at agriculture could have spared them the horrors they now faced. They knew it, but they were not about to admit it. How much easier it was simply to accuse the Americans of failing to give them proper aid; how much simpler to accept the Russian panacea.

And then there was the general worsening of relations between the United States and the UDCs. Many things had contributed to this. The situation in America in the first half of the 1970's deserves our close scrutiny. Being more dependent on imports for raw materials than the Soviet Union, the United States had, in the early 1970's, adopted more and more heavy-handed policies in order to insure continuing supplies. Military adventures in Asia and Latin America had further lessened the international credibility of the United States as a great defender of freedom—an image which had begun to deteriorate rapidly during the pointless and fruitless Viet-Nam conflict. At home, acceptance of the carefully manufactured image lessened dramatically, as even the more romantic and chauvinistic citizens began to understand the role of the military and the industrial system in what John Kenneth Galbraith had aptly named "The New Industrial State."

At home in the USA the early '70s were traumatic times. Racial violence grew and the habitability of the cities diminished, as nothing substantial was done to ameliorate either racial inequities or urban blight. Welfare rolls grew as automation and general technological progress forced more and more people into the category of "unemployable." Simultaneously a taxpayers' revolt occurred. Although there was not enough money to build the schools, roads, water systems, sewage systems, jails, hopsitals, urban transit lines, and all the other amenities needed to support a burgeoning population, Americans refused to tax themselves more heavily. Starting in Youngstown, Ohio in 1969 and followed closely by Richmond, California, community after community was forced to close its schools or curtail educational operations for lack of funds. Water supplies, already marginal in quality and quantity in many places by 1970, deteriorated quickly. Water rationing occurred in 1723 municipalities in the summer of 1974, and hepatitis and epidemic dysentery rates climbed about 500 per cent between 1970-1974.

[III]

Air pollution continued to be the most obvious manifestation of environmental deterioration. It was, by 1972, quite literally in the eyes of all Americans. The year 1973 saw not only the New York and Los Angeles smog disasters, but also the publication of the Surgeon General's massive report on air pollution and health. The public had been partially prepared for the worst by the publicity given to the U.N. pollution conference held in 1972. Deaths in the late '60s caused by smog were well known to scientists, but the public had ignored them because they mostly involved the early demise of the old and sick rather than people dropping dead on the freeways. But suddenly our citizens were faced with nearly 200,000 corpses and massive documentation that they could be the next to die from respiratory disease. They were not ready for that scale of disaster. After all, the U.N. conference had not predicted that accumulated air pollution would make the planet uninhabitable until almost 1990. The population was terrorized as TV screens became filled with scenes of horror from the disaster areas. Especially vivid was NBC's coverage of hundreds of unattended people choking out their lives outside of New York's hospitals. Terms like nitrogen oxide, acute bronchitis and cardiac arrest began to have real meaning for most Americans.

The ultimate horror was the announcement that chlorinated hydrocarbons were now a major constituent of air pollution in all American cities. Autopsies of smog disaster victims revealed an average chlorinated hydrocarbon load in fatty tissue equivalent to 26 parts per million of DDT. In October, 1973, the Department of Health, Education and Welfare announced studies which showed unequivocally that increasing death rates from hypertension, cirrhosis of the liver, liver cancer and a series of other diseases had resulted from the chlorinated hydrocarbon load. They estimated that Americans born since 1946 (when DDT usage began) now had a life expectancy of only 49 years, and predicted that if current patterns continued, this expectancy would reach 42 years by 1980, when it might level out. Plunging insurance stocks triggered a stock market panic. The president of Velsicol, Inc., a major pesticide producer, went on television to "publicly eat a teaspoonful of DDT" (it was really powdered milk) and announce that HEW had been infiltrated by Communists. Other giants of the petrochemical industry, attempting to dispute the indisputable evidence, launched a massive pressure campaign on Congress to force HEW to "get out of agriculture's business." They were aided by the agro-chemical journals, which had decades of experience in misleading the public about the benefits and dangers of pesticides. But by now the public realized that it had been duped. The Nobel Prize for medicine and physiology was given to Drs. J. L. Radomski and W. B. Deichmann, who in the late 1960's had pioneered in the documentation of the long-term lethal effects of chlorinated hydrocarbons. A Presidential Commission with unimpeachable credentials directly accused the agro-chemical complex of "condemning many millions of Americans to an early death." The year 1973 was the year in which Americans finally came to understand the direct threat to their existence posed by environmental deterioration.

And 1973 was also the year in which most people finally comprehended the indirect threat. Even the president of Union Oil Company and several other industrialists publicly stated their concern over the reduction of bird populations which had resulted from

pollution by DDT and other chlorinated hydrocarbons. Insect populations boomed because they were resistant to most pesticides and
had been freed, by the incompetent use of those pesticides, from
most of their natural enemies. Rodents swarmed over crops, multi-
plying rapidly in the absence of predatory birds. The effect of pests
on the wheat crop was especially disastrous in the summer of 1973,
since that was also the year of the great drought. Most of us can
remember the shock which greeted the announcement by atmospheric physicists that the shift of the jet stream which had caused
the drought was probably permanent. It signalled the birth of the
Midwestern desert. Man's air-polluting activities had by then
caused gross changes in climatic patterns. The news, of course,
played hell with commodity and stock markets. Food prices skyrocketed, as savings were poured into hoarded canned goods. Official assurances that food supplies would remain ample fell on deaf
ears, and even the government showed signs of nervousness when
California migrant field workers went out on strike again in protest
against the continued use of pesticides by growers. The strike bur-
geoned into farm burning and riots. The workers, calling themselves
"The Walking Dead," demanded immediate compensation for their
shortened lives, and crash research programs to attempt to lengthen
them.

It was in the same speech in which President Edward Kennedy,
after much delay, finally declared a national emergency and called
out the National Guard to harvest California's crops, that the first
mention of population control was made. Kennedy pointed out that
the United States would no longer be able to offer any food aid to
other nations and was likely to suffer food shortages herself. He
suggested that, in view of the manifest failure of the Green Revolution, the only hope of the UDCs lay in population control. His
statement, you will recall, created an uproar in the underdeveloped
countries. Newspaper editorials accused the United States of wish-
ing to prevent small countries from becoming large nations and thus
threatening American hegemony. Politicians asserted that President Kennedy was a "creature of the giant drug combine" that
wished to shove its pills down every woman's throat.

Among Americans, religious opposition to population control
was very slight. Industry in general also backed the idea. Increasing
poverty in the UDCs was both destroying markets and threatening

supplies of raw materials. The seriousness of the raw material situation had been brought home during the Congressional Hard Resources hearings in 1971. The exposure of the ignorance of the cornucopian economists had been quite a spectacle—a spectacle brought into virtually every American's home in living color. Few would forget the distinguished geologist from the University of California who suggested that economists be legally required to learn at least the most elementary facts of geology. Fewer still would forget that an equally distinguished Harvard economist added that they might be required to learn some economics, too. The overall message was clear: America's resource situation was bad and bound to get worse. The hearings had led to a bill requiring the Departments of State, Interior, and Commerce to set up a joint resource procurement council with the express purpose of "insuring that proper consideration of American resource needs be an integral part of American foreign policy."

Suddenly the United States discovered that it had a national consensus: population control was the only possible salvation of the underdeveloped world. But that same consensus led to heated debate. How could the UDCs be persuaded to limit their populations, and should not the United States lead the way by limiting its own? Members of the intellectual community wanted America to set an example. They pointed out that the United States was in the midst of a new baby boom: her birth rate, well over 20 per thousand per year, and her growth rate of over one per cent per annum were among the very highest of the developed countries. They detailed the deterioration of the American physical and psychic environments, the growing health threats, the impending food shortages, and the insufficiency of funds for desperately needed public works. They contended that the nation was clearly unable or unwilling to properly care for the people it already had. What possible reason could there be, they queried, for adding any more? Besides, who would listen to requests by the United States for population control when that nation did not control her own profligate reproduction?

Those who opposed population controls for the U.S. were equally vociferous. The military-industrial complex, with its all-too-human mixture of ignorance and avarice, still saw strength and prosperity in numbers. Baby food magnates, already worried by the growing nitrate pollution of their products, saw their market disappearing. Steel manufacturers saw a decrease in aggregate demand and slippage for that holy of holies, the Gross National Product. And military men saw, in the growing population-food-environment crisis, a serious threat to their carefully nurtured Cold War. In the end, of course, economic arguments held sway, and the "inalienable right of every American couple to determine the size of its family," a freedom invented for the occasion in the early '70s, was not compromised.

The population control bill, which was passed by Congress early in 1974, was quite a document, nevertheless. On the domestic front, it authorized an increase from 100 to 150 million dollars in funds for "family planning" activities. This was made possible by a general feeling in the country that the growing army on welfare needed family planning. But the gist of the bill was a series of measures designed to impress the need for population control on the UDCs. All American aid to countries with overpopulation problems was required by law to consist in part of population control assistance. In order to receive any assistance each nation was required not only to accept the population control aid, but also to match it according to a complex formula. "Overpopulation" itself was defined by a formula based on U.N. statistics, and the UDCs were required not only to accept aid, but also to show progress in reducing birth rates. Every five years the status of the aid program for each nation was to be re-evaluated.

The reaction to the announcement of this program dwarfed the response to President Kennedy's speech. A coalition of UDCs attempted to get the U.N. General Assembly to condemn the United States as a "genetic aggressor." Most damaging of all to the American cause was the famous "25 Indians and a dog" speech by Mr. Shankarnarayan, Indian Ambassador to the U.N. Shankarnarayan pointed out that for several decades the United States, with less than six per cent of the people of the world had consumed roughly 50 per cent of the raw materials used every year. He described vividly America's contribution to worldwide environmental deterioration, and he scathingly denounced the miserly record of United States foreign aid as "unworthy of a fourth-rate power, let alone the most powerful nation on earth."

It was the climax of his speech, however, which most historians claim once and for all destroyed the image of the United States.

Shankarnarayan informed the assembly that the average American family dog was fed more animal protein per week than the average Indian got in a month. "How do you justify taking fish from protein-starved Peruvians and feeding them to your animals?" he asked. "I contend," he concluded, "that the birth of an American baby is a greater disaster for the world than that of 25 Indian babies." When the applause had died away, Mr. Sorensen, the American representative, made a speech which said essentially that "other countries look after their own self-interest, too." When the vote came, the United States was condemned.

[IV]

This condemnation set the tone of U.S.-UDC relations at the time the Russian Thanodrin proposal was made. The proposal seemed to offer the masses in the UDCs an opportunity to save themselves and humiliate the United States at the same time; and in human affairs, as we all know, biological realities could never interfere with such an opportunity. The scientists were silenced, the politicians said yes, the Thanodrin plants were built, and the results were what any beginning ecology student could have predicted. At first Thanodrin seemed to offer excellent control of many pests. True, there was a rash of human fatalities from improper use of the lethal chemical, but, as Russian technical advisors were prone to note, these were more than compensated for by increased yields. Thanodrin use skyrocketed throughout the underdeveloped world. The Mikoyan design group developed a dependable, cheap agricultural aircraft which the Soviets donated to the effort in large numbers. MIG sprayers became even more common in UDCs than MIG interceptors.

Then the troubles began. Insect strains with cuticles resistant to Thanodrin penetration began to appear. And as streams, rivers, fish culture ponds and onshore waters became rich in Thanodrin, more fisheries began to disappear. Bird populations were decimated. The sequence of events was standard for broadcast use of a synthetic pesticide: great success at first, followed by removal of natural enemies and development of resistance by the pest. Populations of crop-eating insects in areas treated with Thanodrin made steady comebacks and soon became more abundant than ever. Yields plunged, while farmers in their desperation increased the Thanodrin dose and shortened the time between treatments. Death from Thanodrin poisoning became common. The first violent incident occurred in the Canete Valley of Peru, where farmers had suffered a similar chlorinated hydrocarbon disaster in the mid-'50s. A Russian advisor serving as an agricultural pilot was assaulted and killed by a mob of enraged farmers in January, 1978. Trouble spread rapidly during 1978, especially after the word got out that two years earlier Russia herself had banned the use of Thanodrin at home because of its serious effects on ecological systems. Suddenly Russia, and not the United States, was the *bête noir* in the UDCs. "Thanodrin parties" became epidemic, with farmers, in their ignorance, dumping carloads of Thanodrin concentrate into the sea. Russian advisors fled, and four of the Thanodrin plants were leveled to the ground. Destruction of the plants in Rio and Calcutta led to hundreds of thousands of gallons of Thanodrin concentrate being dumped directly into the sea.

Mr. Shankarnarayan again rose to address the U.N., but this time it was Mr. Potemkin, representative of the Soviet Union, who was on the hot seat. Mr. Potemkin heard his nation described as the greatest mass killer of all time as Shankarnarayan predicted at least 30 million deaths from crop failures due to overdependence on Thanodrin. Russia was accused of "chemical aggression," and the General Assembly, after a weak reply by Potemkin, passed a vote of censure.

It was in January, 1979, that huge blooms of a previously unknown variety of diatom were reported off the coast of Peru. The blooms were accompanied by a massive die-off of sea life and of the pathetic remainder of the birds which had once feasted on the anchovies of the area. Almost immediately another huge bloom was reported in the Indian ocean, centering around the Seychelles, and then a third in the South Atlantic off the African coast. Both of these were accompanied by spectacular die-offs of marine animals. Even more ominous were growing reports of fish and bird kills at oceanic points where there were no spectacular blooms. Biologists were soon able to explain the phenomena: the diatom had evolved an enzyme which broke down Thanodrin; that enzyme also produced a breakdown product which interfered with the transmission of nerve impulses, and was therefore lethal to animals. Unfortunately, the biologists could suggest no way of repressing the poisonous diatom bloom in time. By September, 1979, all important animal life in the sea was extinct. Large areas of coastline had to be evacuated, as windrows of dead fish created a monumental stench.

But stench was the least of man's problems. Japan and China were faced with almost instant starvation from a total loss of the seafood on which they were so dependent. Both blamed Russia for their situation and demanded immediate mass shipments of food. Russia had none to send. On October 13, Chinese armies attacked Russia on a broad front. . . .

[V]

A pretty grim scenario. Unfortunately, we're a long way into it already. Everything mentioned as happening before 1970 has actually occurred; much of the rest is based on projections of trends already appearing. Evidence that pesticides have long-term lethal effects on human beings has started to accumulate, and recently Robert Finch, Secretary of the Department of Health, Education and Welfare expressed his extreme apprehension about the pesticide situation. Simultaneously the petrochemical industry continues its unconscionable poison-peddling. For instance, Shell Chemical has been carrying on a high-pressure campaign to sell the insecticide Azodrin to farmers as a killer of cotton pests. They continue their program even though they know that Azodrin is not only ineffective, but often *increases* the pest density. They've covered themselves nicely in an advertisement which states, "Even if an overpowering migration [sic] develops, the flexibility of Azodrin lets you regain control fast. Just increase the dosage according to label recommendations." It's a great game—get people to apply the poison and kill the natural enemies of the pests. Then blame the increased pests on "migration" and sell even more pesticide!

Right now fisheries are being wiped out by over-exploitation, made easy by modern electronic equipment. The companies producing the equipment know this. They even boast in advertising that only their equipment will keep fishermen in business until the final kill. Profits must obviously be maximized in the short run. Indeed, Western society is in the process of completing the rape and murder of the planet for economic gain. And, sadly, most of the rest of the world is eager for the opportunity to emulate our behavior. But the underdeveloped peoples will be denied that opportunity—the days of plunder are drawing inexorably to a close.

Most of the people who are going to die in the greatest cataclysm in the history of man have already been born. More than three and a half billion people already populate our moribund globe, and about half of them are hungry. Some 10 to 20 million will starve to death *this year*. In spite of this, the population of the earth will increase by 70 million souls in 1969. For mankind has artificially lowered the death rate of the human population, while in general birth rates have remained high. With the input side of the population system in high gear and the output side slowed down, our fragile planet has filled with people at an incredible rate. It took several million years for the population to reach a total of two billion people in 1930, while a *second two billion will have been added by 1975!* By that time some experts feel that food shortages will have escalated the present level of world hunger and starvation into famines of unbelievable proportions. Other experts, more optimistic, think the ultimate food-population collision will not occur until the decade of the 1980's. Of course more massive famine may be avoided if other events cause a prior rise in the human death rate.

Both worldwide plague and thermonuclear war are made more probable as population growth continues. These, along with famine, make up the trio of potential "death rate solutions" to the population problem—solutions in which the birth rate-death rate imbalance is redressed by a rise in the death rate rather than by a lowering of the birth rate. Make no mistake about it, *the imbalance will be redressed*. The shape of the population growth curve is one familiar to the biologist. It is the outbreak part of an outbreak-crash sequence. A population grows rapidly in the presence of abundant resources, finally runs out of food or some other necessity, and crashes to a low level or extinction. Man is not only running out of food, he is also destroying the life support systems of the Spaceship Earth. The situation was recently summarized very succinctly: "It is the top of the ninth inning. Man, always a threat at the plate, has been hitting Nature hard. It is important to remember, however, that NATURE BATS LAST."

The Eco-Establishment

Katherine Barkley
and Steve Weissman

Ask Vietnam protesters about the April 22 National Environmental Teach-In and they'll tell you it's a scheme to contain their spring offensive against the ecological disaster in Southeast Asia. Ask young blacks about this new movement to save the ecosystem and they'll tell you that it is a way of distracting attention from the old movement that was supposed to save their skins.

Then go and talk to an environmental activist, a Survival Walker. Ask him why the ecology movement has turned its back on Vietnam and civil rights and he'll explain, with a convincing freshness the old New Left has lost, that the sky is falling. He'll point out that we all have to breathe and that none of us—white or black, Vietnamese peasant or American marine—has much of a future on CO_2. We all must eat, and a diet of pesticides is deadly. We all need water, and the dwindling supplies are unfit for human (or even industrial) consumption. We all depend on the same limited forests, mines, oceans and soil, and we are all going to choke on the same waste and pollution.

To this new ecology activist, nothing could be more obvious: we've all got to unite behind the overriding goal of unfouling our common nest before it's too late, turning back the pages of the environmental doomsday book. If we succeed, then we can get back to these other questions. There is no stopping, he will add, an idea whose time has come.

He will be right, too—though a bit naive about where ideas come from and where movements go. Environment *will be* the issue of the '70's, but not simply because the air got thicker or the oceans less bubbly, or even because the war in Vietnam got too bloody to have to think about every day. It will be the issue of the '70's

15

because such stewards of the nation's wealth as the Ford Foundation, with its Resources for the Future, Inc. (RFF), and Laurance Rockefeller's Conservation Foundation needed a grass-roots movement to help consolidate their control over national policy-making, bolster their hold over world resources, and escalate further cycles of useless economic growth.

[II]

The environment bandwagon is not as recent a phenomenon as it seems. It began to gather momentum back in the mid-'60's under the leadership of Resources for the Future. "The relationship of people to resources, which usually has been expressed in terms of quantity, needs to be restated for modern times to emphasize what is happening to the quality of resources," warned RFF President Joseph L. Fisher in his group's 1964 report. "The wide variety of threats to the quality of the environment may well embrace the gravest U.S. resources problem for the next generation." The following year, Resources for the Future established a special research and educational program in environmental quality, funded with a $ 1.1 million grant from its parent organization, the Ford Foundation.

Created by Ford in the early '50's during the scare over soaring materials costs, RFF had just made its name in conservation by organizing the Mid-Century Conference on Resources for the Future, the first major national conservation conference since Teddy Roosevelt and Gifford Pinchot staged the National Governors' Conference in 1908. Held in 1953, the Mid-Century Conference mustered broad support from both the country's resource users and conservers for the national conservation policy already spelled out by President Truman's Materials Policy Commission. It was this Commission, headed by William S. Paley (board chairman of CBS and a founding director of RFF), which had openly affirmed the nation's inalienable right to extract cheap supplies of raw materials from the underdeveloped countries, and which set the background for Eisenhower and Dulles' oft-quoted concern over the fate of the tin and tungsten of Southeast Asia. Insuring adequate supplies of resources for the future became a conservationist byword.

By the mid-'60's, Resources for the Future had begun to broaden its concern to include resource quality, thus setting the tone for a decade of conservationist rhetoric and behavior. The trustees of the Ford Foundation, an executive committee of such international resource users and polluters as Esso and Ford Motor, established a separate Resources and Environment Division which, since 1966, has nourished such groups as Open Space Action Committee, Save-the-Redwoods League, Massachusetts Audubon Society, Nature Conservancy, and the Environmental Defense Fund. A year later, the Rockefeller Foundation set up an Environmental Studies Division, channelling money to the National Academy of Science and RFF and to Laurance Rockefeller's own pet project, the Conservation Foundation.

The conservationist-planners' new concern over threats to the quality of resources, and to life itself, was actually an outgrowth of their earlier success in assuring cheap and plentiful raw materials. It had become clear that supplies of resources would be less a problem than the immense amount of waste generated as a by-product of those now being refined. The more industry consumed, the more it produced and sold, the larger and more widespread the garbage dumps. Rivers and lakes required costly treatment to make water suitable for use in homes and industry. Smoggy air corroded machines, ruined timberlands, reduced the productivity of crop lands and livestock—to say nothing of its effect on the work capacity of the average man. Pesticides were killing more than pests, and raising the spectre of cumulative disaster. Cities were getting noisier, dirtier, uglier and more tightly packed, forcing the middle class to the suburbs and the big urban landowners to the wall. "Ugliness," Lyndon Johnson exlaimed sententiously, "is costly."

This had long been obvious to the conservationists. Something had to be done, and the elite resource planners took as their model for action the vintage 1910 American conservation movement, especially its emphasis on big business cooperation with big government.

[III]

When the 1890 census officially validated the fact that the frontier was closed, a generation of business and government leaders realized with a start that the American Eden had its bounds. Land, timber and water were all limited, as was the potential for conflicts over their apportionment. What resources should timbermen, grazers or farmers exploit? What should be preserved as a memory of the American past? Who would decide these questions? The conservationists—Teddy Roosevelt, Chief Forester Gifford Pinchot and some of the bigger timber, grazing and agricultural interests—pushed heavily for a new policy to replace the crude and wanton pillage which had been part of the frontier spirit. While preservationists like John Muir were fighting bitterly against any and all use of wild areas by private interests, the conservationists wanted only to make sure that the environment would be exploited with taste and efficiency.

Roosevelt and his backers won out, of course. And the strategy they used is instructive: failing initially to muster congressional support for their plan, they mobilized a broadly based conservation movement, supposedly to regulate the private interests which they in fact represented. Backed by the widespread public support it had whipped up, the conservationist juggernaut then began to move the country toward a more regulated—but still private—exploitation of its riches.

Of course, the private interests which had helped draft this policy also moved—to staff the regulatory agencies, provide jobs for retiring regulators, and generally to put the right man in the right niche most of the time. Within short order, the regulatory agencies were captives of the interests they were supposed to regulate, and they were soon being used as a screen which kept the public from seeing the way that small interests were squeezed out of the competition for resources. Their monopoly position thus strengthened by regulatory agencies, these large interests found it easy to pass the actual costs of regulation on to the citizen consumer.

[IV]

The old American conservation movement had reacted out of fear over resource scarcities; the new movement of the mid-'60's feared, as well, the destruction of resource quality. And the corporation conservationists and their professional planners in organizations like Resources for the Future once again looked to government regulations as an answer to the difficulties they foresaw. Only this time the stakes were much higher than they had been at the early part of the century. Many of the resource planners want an all-encompassing environmental agency or Cabinet level Department of Resources, Environment and Population. Holding enormous power over a wide range of decisions, this coordinating apparatus would be far more convenient for the elite than the present array of agencies, each influenced by its own interest groups.

Who will benefit from this increased environmental consciousness and who will pay is already quite clear to business, if not to most young ecology activists. "The elite of business leadership," reports Fortune, "strongly desire the federal government to step in, set the standards, regulate all activities pertaining to the environment, and help finance the job with tax incentives." The congressional background paper for the 1968 hearings on National Policy on Environmental Quality, prepared with the help of Rockefeller's Conservation Foundation, spells out the logic in greater detail: "Lack of national policy for the environment has now become as expensive to the business community as to the Nation at large. In most enterprises, a social cost can be carried without undue burden if all competitors carry it alike. For example, industrial waste disposal costs can, like other costs of production, be reflected in prices to consumers. But this becomes feasible only when public law and administration put all comparable forms of waste-producing enterprises under the same requirements." Only the truly powerful could be so candid about their intention to pick the pocket of the consumer to pay for the additional costs they will be faced with.

The resource planners are also quite frank about the wave of subsidies they expect out of the big clean-up campaign. "There will have to be a will to provide funds," explains Joseph Fisher, "to train the specialists, do the research and experimentation, build the laws and institutions through which more rapid progress [in pollution control] can be made, and of course, build the facilities and equipment." The coming boondoggles—replete with tax incentives, direct government grants, and new products—will make the oil depletion allowance seem tame. And what's more, it will be packaged as a critical social service.

The big business conservationists will doubtless be equally vocal about the need for new bond issues for local water and sewage treatment facilities; lead crusades to overcome reluctance of the average citizen to vote "yes" on bond measures; and then, as bond-holders themselves, skim a nice tax-free six or seven per cent off the top.

It isn't just the citizen and taxpayer who will bear the burden, however. Bedraggled Mother Nature, too, will pay. Like the original conservation movement it is emulating, today's big business conservation is not interested in preserving the earth; it is rationally reorganizing for a more efficient rape of resources (e.g., the export of chemical-intensive agribusiness) and the production of an even grosser national product.

The seeming contradictions are mind-boggling: industry is combating waste so it can afford to waste more; it is planning to produce more (smog-controlled) private autos to crowd more high-ways, which means even more advertising to create more "needs" to be met by planned obsolescence. Socially, the result is disastrous. Ecologically, it could be the end.

Why don't the businessmen simply stop their silly growthmanship? They can't. If one producer slowed down in the mad race, he'd be eaten up by his competitors. If all conspired together to restrain growth permanently, the unemployment and cutbacks would make today's recession look like full employment, and the resulting unrest would make today's dissent look like play time at Summerhill.

[V]

They began in the mid-'60's in low key, mobilizing the academicians, sprinkling grants and fellowships at the "better" schools, and coordinating research efforts of Resources for the Future, the Conservation Foundation, RAND, Brookings Institution, the National Academy of Science and the Smithsonian Institution. Major forums were held in 1965 and 1966 on "The Quality of the Environment" and "Future Environments of North America." Research findings were programmed directly into industrial trade associations and business firms.

Then the resource people put their men and programs in the official spotlight: Laurance Rockefeller (founder of and major donor to the Conservation Foundation and also a director of RFF) chaired both the White House Conference on Natural Beauty and the Citizens' Advisory Committee on Recreation and Natural Beauty (which Nixon has rechristened his Citizens' Advisory Committee on Environmental Quality). Conservation Foundation President Russell Train headed up Nixon's Task Force on Resources and Environment, with help from Fisher and several other directors of RFF and the Conservation Foundation, and then became Undersecretary of Interior.

Then the media were plugged in, an easy task for men who have in their hands the direction of CBS, National Educational Television, Time-Life-Fortune, Christian Science Monitor, New York Times and Cowles publications, as well as many of the trade journals and conservation magazines. Independent media, seeing that environment was now news, picked up and broadcast the studies which the conservation elite had produced. Public opinion leaders told their public, in Business Week's words, "to prepare for the approval of heavy public and private spending to fight pollution."

Finally, the grass roots wery given the word. RFF, Ford and Rockefeller had long worked with and financed the old-time conservation groups, from Massachusetts Audubon to the Sierra Club, and now the big money moved beyond an appreciation of wilderness to a greater activism. When, for example, David Brower broke with the Sierra Club, it was Robert O. Anderson of Atlantic-Richfield and RFF who gave him $200,000 to set up Friends of the Earth (prudently channeling the donation through the organization's tax-exempt affiliate, the John Muir Institute).

When Senator Gaylord Nelson and Congressman Pete McCloskey got around to pushing the National Teach-In, it was the Conservation Foundation, the Audubon Society and the American Conservation Association which doled out the money while Friends of the Earth was putting together *The Environmental Handbook*, meant to be the Bible of the new movement.

The big business conservationists and their professionals didn't buy off the movement; they built it.

[VI]

Ecology activists out picketing a polluter or cleaning up a creek will have total freedom to make up their own minds about the threats to our environment, and they will have every right to choose their own course of constructive action. Yet they will surely never get a dime from Robert Anderson, or even a farthing from Ford or Rockefeller. And so far, the grass-roots ecology movement has done nothing but echo the eco-elite.

Ecology, unlike most of the fractured scientific field, is holistic. It talks of life and its environment as a totality: how organisms relate to each other and to the system which provides their life-support system. As a discipline applied to human affairs, then, ecology should help us get a whole view of our natural and social environment—from oxygen cycles to business cycles, from the jeopardized natural environment to the powerful institutional environment which creates that jeopardy. If it revealed these inter-connections, ecology would become, as it has been called, a "sub-versive science," subverting the polluters and resource-snatchers who now control the conservation of the nation's wealth. It would point the finger not simply at profit-making polluters or greedy consumers, but at the great garbage-creation system itself—the corporate capitalist economy.

But this is a far cry from the ecology movement as we have inherited it. Ecology, the science of interconnections, becomes a matter of cleaning up beaches and trying to change individuals' habits and attitudes, while ignoring the institutions which created them and practically all environmental damage.

The grass-roots ecology groups do have politics—the politics of consumer boycotts, shareholder democracy and interest group pluralism, all of which show a wonderfully anachronistic faith in the fairness of the market, political and economic. "If Dow pollutes," say the boycotters, "then we just won't buy Saran Wrap." If Super Suds won't make biodegradable soap, we'll buy Ivory. If Ford and Chevy won't make steam cars, we'll buy Japanese imports. From the planned obsolescence in automobiles, to 20 brands of toothpaste, much of what inudstry produces is insulting to the intelligence while also serving no real need; it is waste, to say nothing of the enormous pollution entailed in overproduction.

Consumer sovereignty has gone the way of the dodo, its passing noted two decades back by that stalwart defender of the new corporate capitalism, John Kenneth Galbraith. Consumers just don't control what gets produced, or how. To educate or build support for some stronger action, boycotts, like the picket line, work well. But to change production habits, an ecology movement will really have to pull the big plug at the other end of the TV transmitter, or better, at the production line itself.

Failing in the economic arena, the ecology groups can of course try their hand directly in the political marketplace. Oil has its lobby, the auto manufacturers theirs. Why not a People's Lobby? Californians have already created one, which is now pushing in Sacramento for a referendum "to make the polluters pay." The Environmental Defense League, geared primarily to the court system, is also defending the environment in Congress. The Sierra Club has already lost its tax-exempt status for being too political, and a number of the older conservation groups are pushing new, streamlined legislation. The strategy seems to be paying off, winning victories here and there. Most of the victories, however, merely strengthen the regulatory agencies, which, after public vigilance peters out, will become tools of the big corporations.

Where boycotts and stockholder strategies simply fail, the interest group politics may lead the ecology movement off the edge of a very well-conserved cliff. Eco-catastrophe threatens to kill us all—and Mother Nature, too. But to engage in the give-and-take of interest group politics, the ecologists must grant serious consideration to and must compromise with the oil interests, auto manufacturers and other powerful business groups. Standard Oil gets Indonesia only if they will market that country's prized sulphur-free oil here; the auto makers can keep producing their one-man-one-car civilization in return for making additional profit (and apparent compromise) on smog control. The world is dying: write your congressman today.

From lobbying, the eco-groups will move into the nearest election, trying to put Paul Ehrlich or David Brower in office. But elections aren't won on single issues. Allies must be wooed, coalitions built. Already parochial and out of sympathy with the blacks and other out-groups, the environmentalists, anxious to infiltrate the electoral system, will become even more respectable and more careful to avoid contamination by "extreme" positions or people. They will become further compartmentalized and will be at dead center, sacrificing even those of their own who refuse to compromise.

Avoiding "politics," the ecologists have taken up the old liberal shuck. Give equal freedom to aristocrats and the people, to bosses and workers, to landlords and tenants, and let both sides win. The scheme, of course, overlooks the one-sided distribution of resources, money and media-power. Some "reformers" will have all they need, but their solution, which will become *the* solution, is itself a good part of the problem. Profit-seekers and growth-mongers can't co-exist with Mother Nature and her fragile children without doing them irreparable harm.

To save any semblance of democracy, a decent relationship to the environment and perhaps the environment itself—ecology, the "in" movement, must become a movement of the outs. It must be committed to a long-term militant fight on more clearly understood grounds—its *own* grounds. That too might be impossible. But, as Eugene V. Debs once observed, it's a lot better to fight for what you want and not get it, than to fight for—and get—what you don't want.

Katherine Barkley is a staff member of the Pacific Studies Center.

Is a Rockefeller Baby

Steve Weissman

Paul Ehrlich is a nice man. He doesn't hate blacks, advocate genocide or defend the empire. He simply believes that the world has too many people and he's ready at the drop of a diaper pin to say so. He's written his message in *The Population Bomb,* lectured it in universities and churches, and twice used America's own form of birth control, the late-night Johnny Carson Show, to regale bleary-eyed moms and dads with tales of a standing-room-only world, a time of famines, plague and pestilence.

Together with Berkeley's Kingsley Davis and Santa Barbara's Garrett Hardin, Ehrlich represents a newly-popular school of academics out to make overpopulation the central menace of our age. Except for a still hesitant Pope, their crusade seems sure of success. Everyone from Arthur Godfrey to beat poet Gary Snyder to the leaders of China's 700,000,000 (whom the populationists alternately ignore and disparage) now agrees that population growth is a problem and that something must be done. The question is *what*? Or, more precisely, *who* will do *what* . . . and to *whom*?

Kingsley Davis, who finds voluntary family planning hopelessly futile, suggests that government postpone the age of marriage. Garrett Hardin in the April 22 Teach-In's *Environmental Handbook* urges mutual coercion mutually agreed upon. Paul Ehrlich wants to eliminate tax exemptions for more than two children, forgetting that the power to tax is the power to destroy. Voluntary family planning is out and population control in, leaving those less kindly disposed to the government to see the gaunt spectre of genocide. Long before even the least of the predicted ecological catastrophes comes to pass, such fears might well turn race on race, young on old, rich on poor.

Ehrlich, recognizing this danger, aims his appeal for smaller families less toward the poor and black than toward the white middle-class American family, which consumes more resources, occupies more space, and creates more waste than any ten of its economic inferiors. But his appeal, while barely denting the great waste-production economy, will only create the self-righteousness to impose America's middle-class will on the world.

We "are going to have to adopt some very tough foreign policy positions," Ehrlich explains, and limiting our own families will let us do that "from a psychologically strong position . . . We must use our political power to push other countries into programs which combine agricultural development and population control." Exactly what kind of power, or whether we would use it globally, or simply in countries which food shipments and "green revolutions" might save from starvation, is unclear. But he hints at a time when we might put temporary sterilants in food and water, while some of his more adventurous colleagues, no doubt impressed by pinpoint bombing in Southeast Asia, would spray whole populations from the air. If we're so willing to napalm peasants to protect them from Communists, we could quite easily use a little sterilant spray to protect them from themselves.

We really needn't speculate, however, Uses of the new overpopulation scare are quite out of the hands of either nice academics average anti-Communist Americans. The same elites and institutions which made America the world's policemen have long been eager to serve as the world's prophylactic and agricultural provisioner, and they are damned grateful to the academics for creating a new humanitarian justification for the age-old game of empire. The academics shouldn't really get the credit though. The heavies had it all planned out back in the '50's, while young Dr. Ehrlich was still studying water snakes in the western end of Lake Erie.

[THE ROCKEFELLER FAMILY PLAN]

In June 1952, John D. Rockefeller III, father of four, eldest grandson of Standard Oil and chairman of tne Rockefeller Foundation, hosted a highly select conference on population in Colonial Williamsburg. To this showpiece of historical conservation, restored by the Rockefellers to its pre-Revolutionary beauty, came some 30 of the nation's most eminent conservationists, public health experts, Planned Parenthood leaders, agriculturalists, demographers and social scientists. After two and a half days of intensive discussion, they agreed to form a new group which could act as "a coordinating and catalytic agent in the broad field of population." The following fall, John D. publicly christened The Population Council and announced that he himself would serve as its first president. With this act of baptism, the population bomb became a Rockefeller baby.

In the decades previous, birth control had been largely small potatoes. The Rockefeller Foundation, together with the Milbank Memorial Fund, had, in 1936, provided John D.'s alma mater, Princeton, with an Office of Population Research. Mississippi, Louisiana, Georgia, Florida and the Carolinas pioneered programs for the (sometimes voluntary) sterilization of the poor. Planned Parenthood, a direct descendant of Margaret Sanger's American Birth Control League, struggled to provide America's poor with free counsel and contraceptives. Guy Irving Burch's Population Reference Bureau, long the leading educator on population dynamics, was little more than a one-man show, as was the Hugh Moore Fund, set up in 1944 by the founder and board chairman of Dixie Cup "to call to the attention of the American Public the dangers inherent in the population explosion."

Once the Rockefellers joined the family, however, family planning became a very different kind of business. The Ford Foundation, Carnegie, the Commonwealth and Community Funds, the Mott Trust and the Mellons joined with John D., his mother, his sister (wife of banker Jean Mauze), his brother and their financial adviser, AEC chairman Lewis Strauss, in pumping fresh blood and money into the Population Council, some of which even trickled over into the Reference Bureau and Planned Parenthood. Wealthy Englishmen and Swedes and their third world associates joined with the Americans in making Planned Parenthood international. The World Bank, headed by Chase National Bank vice president and future Population Council director Eugene Black, put its money behind Princeton's pioneer study on population and economic growth in India. Where birth controllers once went begging, now guest lists at Planned Parenthood banquets and signatures on ubiquitous New York Times ads read like a cross between the Social

Register and Standard and Poor's Directory of Corporation Executives.

This sudden interest of the world's rich in the world's poor, whatever the humanitarian impulse, made good dollars and cents. World War II had exhausted the older colonial empires, and everywhere the cry of nationalism sounded: from Communists in China and Southeast Asia, from neutralists in Indonesia and India, from independence movements in Africa and from economic nationalists in Latin America. People wanted their own steel mills, use of their own oil and iron ore and, most menacing, the right to protect themselves against integration in an international marketplace which systematically favored the already-industrialized.

But the doughty old buzzards of empire were determined to save the species. They would pay deference to the new feelings by encouraging a bit of light industry here, and perhaps even a steel mill there. To give the underdeveloped areas what Nelson Rockefeller termed "a community of interest with us," and to extend control, they would give public loans and foreign aid for roads, dams and schools. Their foundations and universities would train a new class of native managers who, freed from outmoded ideologies, would clearly see that there was more than enough for both rich and poor.

But there wasn't enough, especially not when the post-war export of death-control technology created so many more of the poor. The poor nations rarely came close to providing even the limited economic security which, as in Europe of the Industrial Revolution, would encourage people to give up the traditional peasant security of a large family and permit the population curve to level off. In fact, for much of the population, the newly-expanded money economy actually increased insecurity. Faced with this distortion between fertility and development, developed country elites could see no natural way of stopping population growth. All they could see was people, people, people, each one threatening the hard-won stability which guaranteed access to the world's ores and oil, each one an additional competitor for the use of limited resources.

More people, moreover, meant younger people, gunpowder for more than a mere population explosion. "The restlessness produced in a rapidly growing population is magnified by the preponderance of youth," reported the Rockefeller Fund's overpowering *Prospect for America.* "In a completely youthful population, impatience to realize rising expectations is likely to be pronounced. Extreme nationalism has often been the result."

[HOLDING BACK]

It was to meet these perils of population that the Rockefellers and their kindred joined the family planning movement in such force. But until they had completed a much more thoroughgoing prophylaxis of the new nationalisms, and had worked out an accommodation with Catholic opposition, they were much too sophisticated to preach birth control straight out. That would have sounded far too reminiscent of the older colonialisms and, indirectly, too much like a condemnation of the new pattern of "development."

Consequently, until the spurt of technical assistance in the '60's, the Population Council preached and, within the ideological confines of development thinking, practiced "the scientific study of population problems." They provided fellowships to Americans and, as part of the broader building of native elites, to deserving foreign students. This, they hoped, would build up a cadre of "local personnel," well-studied in population problems, "trained in objective scientific methods and able to interpret the results to their own people." The Council also undertook population studies in the colonies, funded both demographic and medical studies at U.S. universities, worked with international agencies, and maintained its own biomedical lab at Rockefeller Institute. The foundations supplemented this approach, directly funding roughly a dozen major university think-tanks devoted to population studies. These grants no more bought scholars and scholarship than native elites. It was more efficient to rent them. Like Defense Department dollars or direct corporation gifts, the smart population money posed the right (as opposed to the left) questions, paid off for right answers, and provided parameters for scholars interested in "realistic" policy alternatives.

Study, of course, was an apprenticeship for action. By 1957, an "Ad Hoc Committee" of population strategists from the Council, the Rockefeller Fund, Laurance Rockefeller's Conservation Foundation and Planned Parenthood mapped out a full population control program. Published by Population Council President Frederick

Osborn as *Population: An International Dilemma,* the committee's report insisted that population growth, in the rich nations as well as the poor, would become a decisive threat to political stability. To pre-empt such instability, the population planners planned first to win over the educated classes, many of whom themselves felt the threat of population. But, wary of widespread personal sensitivities and nationalist sentiments, they would never push birth control as an end in itself. Instead they would have it grow out of the logical needs of family planning, and leave the task of gaining public acceptance to the native elite, many of whom they had trained.

An even more important antidote to nationalist reaction was the population planners' admission that population was also a problem here in the U.S. "Excessive fertility by families with meager resources must be recognized as one of the potent forces in the perpetuation of slums, ill-health, inadequate education, and even delinquency," the Ad Hoc Committee noted. They were satisfied, however, with the overall "balance of population and resources" in this country and sought only to use tax, welfare and education policy "to equalize births between people at different socio-economic levels" and to "discourage births among the socially handicapped."

[GETTING THE GOVERNMENT IN]

For all their domestic concern, however, population planners were primarily absorbed in "the international dilemma" and the problems of "economic development." Like Walt Rostow, Max Millikan and the authors of the Rockefellers' *Prospect for America,* they emphasized top-down national planning, Western-influenced elites, foreign aid penetration, and the use of economic growth, rather than distribution and welfare, to measure development. As a result, their plan for population bore a scary resemblance to the first Vietnamization which was then recasting the educational system, banking and currency, public works, agriculture, the police, and welfare programs of Vietnam into an American mold.

The population planners' counter to insurgency then entered "official" development thinking in 1959, in the Report of President Eisenhower's Committee to Study the Military Assistance Program. Headed by General William H. Draper II (perhaps best remembered as the American government official who most helped Nazi and Zaibatsu industrialists reconcentrate their power after

World War II), the committee urged that development aid be extended to local maternal and child welfare programs, to the formulation of national population plans, and to additional research on population control.

Ike, a bit old-fashioned about such intimate intervention, flatly refused. He just could not "imagine anything more emphatically a subject that is not a proper political or government activity or function or responsibility . . . This government . . . will not . . . as long as I am here, have a positive policy doctrine in its program that has to do with this problem of birth control. That's not our business."

Business disagreed, the Draper Report became the rallying cry of big business' population movement, and General Draper, an investment banker by trade, headed up both Planned Parenthood's million dollar-a-year World Population Emergency Campaign and even bigger Victor Fund Drive.

The foundations also expanded their own programs. But the Rockefellers, Fords, Draper, and others seemingly born into the population movement hadn't gotten rich by picking up such large tabs; not if they could help it. Despite Ike's sense of propriety, they had continued to press for government sponsorship of birth control —and not without piecemeal gains, even in the Eisenhower government.

When Kennedy became President he agreed to a government role in research, promising to pass requests for birth control information and technical assistance to the foundations, and permitting Deputy Assistant Secretary of State Richard Gardner to make an offer of U.S. family planning aid to the UN.

But none of this satisfied the population people, who, beginning in 1963, made a big public push for major government programs in both domestic and overseas agencies. In May of that year, the blue-ribbon American Assembly, with the help of the Population Council, brought "The Population Dilemma" to a convocation of leaders from all walks of American life. The National Academy of Sciences, assisted professionally and financially by the Council, issued a scary report on *The Growth of World Population.* Draper, Moore, and Harper & Row's Cass Canfield then set up the Population Crisis Committee, "the political action arm of the population control movement," to publish ads, lobby government officials and promote public support for government aid to family planning.

Sometimes the population people defended their proposals on humanitarian grounds; at other times they were more candid: "If the World Bank expects to get its loans repaid by India," explained Draper, "if the U.S., much of whose aid is in the form of loans, expects to have them repaid . . . the population problem . . . must be solved." Bolstered by Fulbright, Gruening and other long-term congressional advocates of "economic development," and by a public reversal of position by former President Eisenhower, the campaign pushed the Kennedy, then the Johnson government closer to open birth control programs.

But fear of domestic controversy, especially in the Catholic community, and a lack of positive foreign response held the movement in check until the White House Conference on International Cooperation, keynoted by John D. Rockefeller III, in November 1965. The Conference Committee on Population—chaired by Gardner and including Black, Canfield, Draper and John D.—then urged that the government greatly expand its birth control assistance to foreign countries. Conference committees on Food and Agriculture and Technical Cooperation and Investment concurred, urging a multilateral approach.

Much impressed by this show of "public support," the very next session of Congress passed Johnson's "New Look" in foreign policy, which made birth control part of foreign assistance and permitted the President to judge a nation's "self-help" in population planning as a criterion for giving Food for Freedom aid. (Separate legislation gave the Department of Health, Education and Welfare a birth control program for domestic consumption.) The "New Look," which combined population control with agricultural development, international education, encouragement of private overseas investment, and multilateral institution-building, was, of course, the response of the mid-'50's to nationalism. It was also a foretaste of what Paul Ehrlich's "tough foreign policy positions" would easily become.

[THE GREEN REVOLUTION]

The new look in intervention got a good test in the Indian famine of '65 and '66—until Biafra the best-advertised famine in recent times, and a major boost for the population control campaign. Ever since the victory of the Chinese Revolution, India has

been a bastion of the "free [enterprise] world." But Western businessmen long fretted over her "neutralism" and "socialism" and
her restrictions on foreign participation in key areas of the economy.

In 1958, India faced a devastating foreign exchange crisis. In
response, the World Bank and the "Aid India Club" promised one
billion dollars a year in aid, and international investors found themselves with golden opportunities. The Ford Foundation quickly
stepped in with a "food crisis" team of experts, which pushed
India's planners into increased agricultural spending, ultimately at
the expense of planned investments in housing and other social services. Several rounds of business conferences on India together with
official and semi-official visits followed until, in 1964, Undersecretary of Commerce Franklin Delano Roosevelt, Jr. led a top-flight
delegation of American business executives to New Delhi with the
explicit objective of "persuading the government to adopt policies
more attractive to potential investors."

Hunger warriors from agribusiness were particularly hot for
expansion. Poor harvest in prior years had driven food prices up,
and with them, the demand for fertilizer and pesticides. Consequently, the Rockefeller's Jersey Standard wanted price and distribution restrictions lifted on their Bombay fertilizer plant. A Bank of
America syndicate, together with India's Birla group, needed
government support for what would become "the largest urea and
compound fertilizer plant in this part of the world." Petroleum
producers, foreseeing an otherwise useless excess of naphtha,
wanted permission to set up fertilizer plants which could utilize the
petroleum by-product. The Ford and Rockefeller foundations
wanted to expand use of their new high yield seeds deliberately bred
for large fertilizer and pesticide inputs, and get on with the commercialization of agriculture.

But Western pressure was of little avail until the failure of the
summer monsoons in 1965. Then, in the words of the World Bank's
Pearson Report, "Instead of signing annual or multiyear [food]
sales agreements, as with other countries and with India itself, in
earlier years, the United States doled out food aid a few months at a
time as policy conditions were agreed upon."

India, faced with a short leash on food supplies, acceded to the foreign pressures. She pared down government control, liberalized her import restriction and devalued the rupee. Her government gave the chemical and oil men permission to build new fertilizer plants, to fix their own prices, to handle their own distribution outside the normal channels of the rural cooperatives, and to maintain a greater share of management control than permitted under Indian law. Most important, officials agreed to give greater emphasis to agriculture and to maintain high food prices as an incentive to growers. "Call them 'strings,' call them 'conditions,' or whatever one likes," boasted the New York Times, "India has little choice now but to agree to many of the terms that the United States, through the World Bank, is putting on its aid. For India simply has nowhere else to turn."

With the ground so carefully prepared, the miracle seeds grew beautifully. Once-barren land flowered. Indian farmers harvested 95 million tons of grain in 1967-68, bettering the best of previous yields by five per cent. The following year they did almost as well, and growers laid plans for 100 million metric tons in 1969-70. Ecstatic Indian government officials announced that India would be self-sufficient in food production by 1971. "The Green Revolution," exclaimed David Rockefeller to the International Industrial Conference, "may ultimately have a cumulative effect in Asia, Africa, and Latin America such as the introduction of the steam engine had in the industrial revolution."

[REVOLUTION OF A DIFFERENT COLOR]

The pressure, bantered about everywhere from the Canarsie Shopping News to Business Week, had been anything but subtle. Profits would be high. Yet even liberals like John Kenneth Galbraith and Chester Bowles, both former ambassadors to New Delhi, lavishly praised the whole enterprise. People have to eat.

They have to, but even with paternalistic green revolutions they still don't always get to. "Modern" agriculture in America and the West, dependent upon high inputs of fertilizer and pesticides, is an ecological disaster. We are only now discovering what DDT and many fertilizers do to our food, water, soil, mother's milk and farm workers. India's prospects are even more bleak. Chemically resistant miracle grains will soon produce miracle pests, which could easily wipe out whole areas. Early high yields depended heavily on unusually good weather—which is not dependable, and on irriga- tion—which is reportedly salting the soil. These problems have led many experts to question how long the revolution will remain green. But most of the experts still come down on the side of more "mod- ern" agriculture, without even exploring possibly safer alternatives like the high-yield, labor-intensive and biologically-integrated "gar- dening" of the best traditional Asian agriculture.

But the real disaster is more immediate. The same high food prices which gave incentive to growers also put sufficient food out of the reach of those who need it most. Commercial agriculture, by definition, produces for profit, not people. At the same time, the new seeds required irrigation and pesticides, and heavy inputs of fertilizer, the costs of which soared with the removal of government price ceilings. "So far," reports Clifton Wharton, Jr., writing in Foreign Affairs, "spectacular results have been achieved primarily among the relatively large commercial farmers." Those who haven't the capital, or can't get the credit from village moneylend- ers or meager government programs, are pushed off their land and into an agricultural proletariat or worse, while the new Kulaks, the peasant capitalists, re-invest their profits in modern labor-saving machinery.

The inevitable result of this trend is class and regional conflict. Wharton reports a clash in the prize Tanjore district of Madras in which 43 persons died in a struggle between landlords and the land- less, "who felt they were not receiving their proper share of the increased prosperity brought by the Green Revolution." Two Swed- ish journalists, Lasse and Lisa Berg, reporting in Stockholm's *Sondagsbilagan,* provide pictures of "excess" Indian peasants burned in kerosene by a landlord. One hates to speculate on how a companion population program would work, but it is all too easy to believe reports from India of forced sterilization.

But there is a positive side. As in the Philippines, where peas- ants displaced by the commercialization of agriculture are strength- ening the Huk resistance, the Green Revolution in India is produc- ing a Red Revolution. For the first time since Independence, mili- tant revolutionary movements have led Indian peasants into rebel- lions in different parts of the country, and in certain areas, the Bergs report, the poorest people in the countryside are organizing themse- lves across the boundaries of caste.

[THE NEW INTERNATIONALISM]

Despite all a Rockefeller might do, the New Look in empire even met obstacles at home. From 1966 on, displeasure with the unwinnable war in Vietnam escalated along with the war-caused inflation, and Congress, though it had authorized the new programs, was increasingly unwilling to fund any new foreign entanglements. In the spring of 1967, for example, Senator Fulbright, impressed with what the White House Conference's Committee on Population had proposed, asked Congress to support voluntary family planning abroad with an appropriation of $50 million a year for three years. His less liberal colleagues approved $35 million for one year. Congress has treated the domestic birth control issue with the same lack of enthusiasm, despite the growth of third world nationalism within the U.S. Members of Congress are just too provincial to understand the needs of empire.

In an attempt to create a congressional climate more favorable to population control, the empire builders decided to drum up some public pressure for their cause. Consequently, a new avalanche of full-page spreads warned war-weary newspaper readers that "The Population Bomb Threatens the Peace of the World"; that "Hungry Nations Imperil the Peace of the World"; that "Whatever your cause, it's a lost cause unless we control population." The ads, sponsored by Hugh Moore's Campaign to Check the Population Explosion and signed by the usual crew of population controllers, urged greatly expanded appropriations and a crash program for population stabilization. A new Presidential Committee on Population and Family Planning, headed by HEW Secretary Wilbur Cohen and, of course, John D. III, persuaded Nixon to promise greatly-expanded federal programs and a commission on domestic population problems. The Ford Foundation, initiating its first grants for birth control assistance in the U.S. in 1966, provided a barrage of money and reports. The American Assembly, with the help of the Kellog Foundation and now-Secretary of Agriculture Clifford Hardin, sponsored a national conference on Overcoming World Hunger which, despite its optimism about the green revolution, continued to push for population control. Hugh Moore pushed Ehrlich's book and his own ads. Draper urged doubling the 1970 AID appropriation for birth control to $100,000 and was warmly applauded by James Riddleberger, his successor as head of the Population Crisis Committee. Environmentalists, along with their enemies, "the industrial polluters," found the chief cause of every problem from slums to suburbs, pollution to protest, in the world's expanding numbers.

More than ever, the population power structure pushed for a world population policy. From the early '50's, the population people realized the sensitivities—religious, ideological, military, political and personal—raised by the offer of birth control assistance, and always advocated international programs. Then, when domestic reaction to intervention in Vietnam soured the overall population control effort, they quickly joined in the generalized elitist move to transfer the entire economic development program to international agencies, where they and their third world friends could directly control the programs without interference from congressional "hicks."

The UN should take the leadership in responding to world population growth. So urged a special United Nations Association panel headed by John D., financed by Ford, and including Richard Gardner, former World Bank president George Woods, former AID administrator and now Ford Director of International Operations David E. Bell, and AID director John A. Hannah. The committee urged the creation of a UN Commissioner of Population with broad powers to coordinate "radically upgraded" population activities. The Commissioner would work under the United Nations Development Program, whose director, Paul Hoffman, is a former president of the Ford Foundation, administrator of the Marshall Plan, and aide to General Draper in the reconquest of Japan by big business. Under Hoffman's guidance, the second UN Decade of Development is already preparing to concentrate on agricultural development, education, and population control.

The American population elite is also trying to beef up the Development Assistance Committee (DAC) of the Organization for Economic Cooperation and Development, which brings together the old Marshall Plan nations with Japan, Australia, Canada and the United States. Since the mid-'60's, DAC has given greater efforts to coordinating the agricultural and population control aid of the members. James Riddleberger, Draper's replacement on the

Population Crisis Committee, was the first chairman of DAC, while the present chairman, former State Department official Edwin Martin, served as a staff member of the original Draper Committee.

Most important in the new internationalism is the World Bank. Headed by Robert McNamara, veteran of population control efforts in Vietnam, the Bank is now developing the management capacity to become the key institution in administering the empire. "Just as McNamara concentrated on the cataclysmal, the nuclear threat, while at the Department of Defense," gushed a New York Times feature, "so at the World Bank he has chosen to make the population explosion, another cataclysmal problem, his central, long-range preoccupation. For if populations are allowed to double every 20 years, as they do in low-income countries, it will wipe out the effect of development and lead to chaos." Aided by former AID administrator William S. Gaud, now executive vice-president of the World Bank's International Finance Corporation, and former Alliance for Progress chief Covey T. Oliver, now U.S. delegate to the World Bank, McNamara is currently preparing for the day when the great statesmen meet to discuss the control of population.

With support in the White House and agreement among their friends (the trustworthy American managers in the international agencies), everything seems to favor the new interventionism of the big business internationlists. Everything, that is, except a new-found popular preference for non-intervention, or even isolation. But if overpopulation per se becomes the new scapegoat for the world's ills, the current hesitations about intervention will fall away. Soon everyone, from the revolting taxpayer who wants to sterilize the Panther-ridden ghettos to the foreign aid addict, will line up behind the World Bank and the UN and join the great international crusade to control the world's population. Let empire save the earth.

Simply fighting this war on people with a people's war will not eliminate the need for each nation to determine how best to balance resources and population. But where there is greater economic security, political participation, elimination of gross class division, liberation of women, and respected leadership, humane and successful population programs are at least possible. Without these conditions, genocide is nicely masked by the welfare imperialism of the

West. In the hands of the self-seeking, humanitarianism is the most terrifying *ism* of all.

_____

Steve Weissman is a member of the Pacific Studies Center in Palo Alto, California. The Center is a research collective specializing in the social, political and economic dimensions of American capitalism. Projects range from studies and publications on U.S. involvement in the Third World, multinational corporations, labor problems, high finance and environmental destruction, to films on ecology and inflation.

_____

Toward an

Ecological Solution

Murray Bookchin

Popular alarm over environmental decay and pollution did not emerge for the first time merely in the late '60's, nor for that matter is it the unique response of the present century. Air pollution, water pollution, food adulteration and other environmental problems were public issues as far back as ancient times, when notions of environmental diseases were far more prevalent than they are today. All of these issues came to the surface again with the Industrial Revolution—a period which was marked by burgeoning cities, the growth of the factory system, and an unprecedented befouling and polluting of air and waterways.

Today the situation is changing drastically and at a tempo that portends a catastrophe for the entire world of life. What is not

Portions of "Metamorphose"   Woodcut by M.C. Escher
Courtesy of the Phoenix Gallery, Berkeley

clearly understood in many popular discussions of the present ecological crisis is that the very nature of the issues has changed, that the decay of the environment is directly tied to the decay of the existing social structure. It is not simply certain malpractices or a given spectrum of poisonous agents that is at stake, but rather the very structure of modern agriculture, industry and the city. Consequently, environmental decay and ecological catastrophe cannot be averted merely by increased programs like "pollution control" which deal with sources rather than systems. To be commensurable to the problem, the solution must entail far-reaching revolutionary changes in society and in man's relation to man.

[I]

To understand the enormity of the ecological crisis and the sweeping transformation it requires, let us briefly revisit the "pollution problem" as it existed a few decades ago. During the 1930's, pollution was primarily a muckraking issue, a problem of expose journalism typified by Kallet and Schlink's "100 Million Guinea Pigs."

This kind of muckraking literature still exists in abundance and finds an eager market among "consumers," that is to say, a public that seeks personal and legislative solutions to pollution problems. Its supreme pontiff is Ralph Nader, an energetic young man who has shrewdly combined traditional muckraking with a safe form of "New Left" activism. In reality, Nader's emphasis belongs to another historical era, for the magnitude of the pollution problem has expanded beyond the most exaggerated accounts of the '30's. The new pollutants are no longer "poisons" in the popular sense of the term; rather they belong to the problems of ecology, not merely pharmacology, and these do not lend themselves to legislative redress.

What now confronts us is not the predominantly specific, rapidly degradable poisons that alarmed an earlier generation, but long-lived carcinogenic and mutagenic agents, such as radioactive isotopes and chlorinated hydrocarbons. These agents become part of the very anatomy of the individual by entering his bone structure, tissues and fat deposits. Their dispersion is so global that they become part of the anatomy of the environment itself. They will be

"Liberation"   Lithograph by M.C. Escher
Courtesy of C.V.S. Roosevelt

within us and around us for years to come, in many cases for generations to come. Their toxic effects are usually chronic rather than acute; the deadly and mutational effects they produce in the individual will not be seen until many years have passed. They are harmful not only in large quantities, but in trace amounts; as such, they are not detectable by human senses or even, in many cases, by conventional methods of analysis. They damage not only specific individuals but the human species as a whole and virtually all other forms of life.

No less alarming is the fact that we must drastically revise our traditional notions of what constitutes an environmental "pollutant." A few decades ago it would have been absurd to describe carbon dioxide and heat as "pollutants" in the customary sense of the term. Yet in both cases they may well rank among the most serious sources of future ecological imbalance and pose major threats to the viability of the planet. As a result of industrial and domestic combustion activities, the quantity of carbon dioxide in the atmosphere has increased by roughly 25 per cent in the past 100 years, a figure that may well double again by the end of the century. The famous "greenhouse effect," which increasing quantities of the gas is expected to produce, has already been widely discussed: eventually, it is supposed, the gas will inhibit the dissipation of the earth's heat into space, causing a rise in overall temperatures which will melt the polar ice caps and result in an inundation of vast coastal areas. Thermal pollution, the result mainly of warm water discharged by nuclear and conventional power plants, has disastrous effects on the ecology of lakes, rivers and estuaries. Increases in water temperature not only damage the physiological and reproductive activities of fish; they also promote the great blooms of algae that have become such formidable problems in waterways.

What is at stake in the ecological crisis we face today is the very capacity of the earth to sustain advanced forms of life. The crisis is being drawn together by massive increases in "typical" forms of air and water pollution; by a mounting accumulation of nondegradable wastes, lead residues, pesticide residues and toxic additives in food; by the expansion of cities into vast urban belts; by increasing stresses due to congestion, noise and mass living; by the wanton scarring of the earth as a result of mining operations, lumbering, and real estate speculation. The result of all this is that the earth within a few decades has been despoiled on a scale that is unprecedented in the entire history of human habitation on the planet.

Finally, the complexity and diversity of life which marked biological evolution over many millions of years is being replaced by a simpler, more synthetic and increasingly homogenized environment. Aside from any esthetic considerations, the elimination of this complexity and diversity may prove to be the most serious loss of all. Modern society is literally undoing the work of organic evolution. If this process continues unabated, the earth may be reduced to a level of biotic simplicity where humanity—whose welfare depends profoundly upon the complex food chains in the soil, on the land surface and in the oceans—will no longer be able to sustain itself as a viable animal species.

"Cartouche"   Woodcut by M.C. Escher
Courtesy of the Vorpal Gallery, San Francisco

[II]

In recent years a type of biological "cold warrior" has emerged who tends to locate the ecological crisis in technology and population growth, thereby divesting it of its explosive social content. Out of this focus has emerged a new version of "original sin" in which tools and machines, reinforced by sexually irresponsible humans, ravage the earth in concert. Both technology and sexual irresponsibility, so the argument goes, must be curbed—if not voluntarily, then by the divine institution called the state.

The naivete of this approach would be risible were it not for its sinister implications. History has known of many different forms of tools and machines, some of which are patently harmful to human welfare and the natural world, others of which have clearly improved the condition of man and the ecology of an area. It would be absurd to place plows and mutagenic defoliants, weaving machines and automobiles, computers and moon rockets, under a common rubric. Worse, it would be grossly misleading to deal with these technologies in a social vacuum.

Technologies consist not only of the devices humans employ to mediate their relationship with the natural world, but also the attitudes associated with these devices. These attitudes are distinctly social products, the results of the social relationships humans establish with each other. What is clearly needed is not a mindless deprecation of technology as such, but rather a reordering and redevelopment of technologies according to ecologically sound principles. We need an eco-technology that will help harmonize society with the natural world.

The same over-simplification is evident in the neo-Malthusian alarm over population growth. The reduction of population growth to a mere ratio between birth rates and death rates obscures the many complex social factors that enter into both statistics. A rising or declining birth rate is not a simple biological datum, any more than is a rising or declining death rate. Both are subject to the influences of the economic status of the individual, the nature of family structure, the values of society, the status of women, the attitude toward children, the culture of the community, and so forth. A change in any single factor interacts with the remainder to produce the statistical data called "birth rate" and "death rate." Culled from such abstract ratios, population growth rates can easily be used to foster authoritarian controls and finally a totalitarian society, especially if neo-Malthusian propaganda and the failure of voluntary birth control are used as an excuse. In arguing that forcible measures of birth control and a calculated policy of indifference to hunger may eventually be necessary to stabilize world populations, the neo-Malthusians are already creating a climate of opinion that will make genocidal policies and authoritarian institutions socially acceptable.

It is supremely ironic that coercion, so clearly implicit in the neo-Malthusian outlook, has acquired a respected place in the public debate on ecology—for the roots of the ecological crisis lie precisely in the coercive basis of modern society. The notion that man must dominate nature emerges directly from the domination of man by man. The patriarchal family may have planted the seed of domination in the nuclear relations of humanity; the classical split between spirit and reality—indeed, mind and labor—may have nourished it; the anti-naturalistic bias of Christianity may have tended to its growth; but it was not until organic community relations, be they tribal, feudal or peasant in form, dissolved into market relationships that the planet itself was reduced to a resource for exploitation.

This centuries-long tendency finds its most exacerbating development in modern capitalism: a social order that is orchestrated entirely by the maxim "Production for the sake of production." Owing to its inherently competitive nature, bourgeois society not only pits humans against each other, but the mass of humanity against the natural world. Just as men are converted into commodities, so every aspect of nature is converted into a commodity, a resource to be manufactured and merchandised wantonly. Entire continental areas in turn are converted into factories, and cities into marketplaces. The liberal euphemisms for these unadorned terms are "growth," "industrial society" and "urban blight." By whatever language they are described, the phenomena have their roots in the domination of man by man.

As technology develops, the maxim "Production for the sake of production" finds its complement in "Consumption for the sake of consumption." The phrase "consumer society" completes the description of the present social order as an "industrial society." Needs are tailored by the mass media to create a public demand for utterly useless commodities, each carefully engineered to deteriorate after a predetermined period of time. The plundering of the human spirit by the marketplace is paralleled by the plundering of the earth by capital. The tendency of the liberal to identify the marketplace with human needs, and capital with technology, represents a calculated error that neutralizes the social thrust of the ecological crisis.

The strategic ratios in the ecological crisis are not the population rates of India but the production rates of the United States, a country that produces more than 50 per cent of the world's goods. Here, too, liberal euphemisms like "affluence" conceal the critical thrust of a blunt word like "waste." With a vast section of its industrial capacity committed to war production, the U.S. is literally trampling upon the earth and shredding ecological links that are vital to human survival. If current industrial projections prove to be accurate, the remaining 30 years of the century will witness a five-fold increase in electric power production, based mostly on nuclear fuels and coal. The colossal burden in radioactive wastes and other effluents that this increase will place on the natural ecology of the earth hardly needs description.

In shorter perspective, the problem is no less disquieting. Within the next five years, lumber production may increase an overall 20 per cent; the output of paper, five per cent annually; folding boxes, three per cent annually; metal cans, four to five per cent annually; plastics (which currently form one to two per cent of municipal wastes), seven per cent annually. Collectively, these industries account for the most serious pollutants in the environment. The utterly senseless nature of modern industrial activity is perhaps best illustrated by the decline in returnable (and reusable) beer bottles from 54 billion bottles in 1960 to 26 billion today. Their place has been taken over by "one-way bottles" (a rise from 8 to 21 billion in the same period) and cans (an increase from 38 to 53 billion). The "one-way bottles" and cans, of course, pose tremendous problems in solid waste disposal, but they do sell better.

It may be that the planet, conceived as a lump of minerals, can

"Three Worlds"   Lithograph by M.C. Escher
Courtesy of the Vorpal Gallery, San Francisco

support these mindless increases in the output of trash. The earth, conceived as a complex web of life, certainly cannot. The only question is, can the earth survive its looting long enough for man to replace the current destructive social system with a humanistic, ecologically oriented society.

The apocalyptic tone that marks so many ecological works over the past decade should not be taken lightly. We are witnessing the end of a world, although whether this world is a long-established social order or the earth as a living organism still remains in question. The ecological crisis, with its threat of human extinction, has developed appositely to the advance of technology, with its promise of abundance, leisure and material security. Both are converging toward a single focus: At a point where the very survival of man is being threatened, the possibility of removing him from the trammels of domination, material scarcity and toil has never been more promising. The very technology that has been used to plunder the planet can now be deployed, artfully and rationally, to make it flourish.

It is necessary to overcome not only bourgeois society but also the long legacy of propertied society: the patriarchal family, the city, the state—indeed, the historic splits that separated mind from sensuousness, individual from society, town from country, work from play, man from nature. The spirit of spontaneity and diversity that permeates the ecological outlook toward the natural world must now be directed toward revolutionary change and utopian reconstruction in the social world. Propertied society, domination, hierarchy and the state, in all their forms, are utterly incompatible with the survival of the biosphere. Either ecology action is revolutionary action or it is nothing at all. Any attempt to reform a social order that by its very nature pits humanity against all the forces of life is a gross deception and serves merely as a safety valve for established institutions.

The application of ecological principles to social reconstruction, on the other hand, opens entirely new opportunities for imagination and creativity. The cities must be decentralized to serve the interests of both natural and social ecology. Urban gigantism is devastating not only to the land, the air, the waterways and the local climate, but to the human spirit. Having reached its limits in the megalopolis—an urban sprawl that can best be described as the "non-city"—the city must be replaced by a multitude of diversified, well-rounded communities, each scaled to human dimensions and to the carrying capacity of its ecosystem. Technology, in turn, must be placed in the service of meaningful human needs, its output gauged to permit a careful recycling of wastes into the environment.

With the community and its technology sculptured to human scale, it should be possible to establish new, diversified energy patterns: the combined use of solar power, wind power and a judicious use of fossil and nuclear fuels. In this decentralized society, a new sense of tribalism, of face-to-face relations, can be expected to

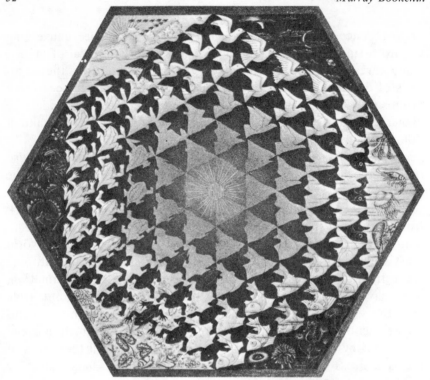

"Verbum"   Lithograph by M.C. Escher
Courtesy of the Vorpal Gallery, San Francisco

replace the bureaucratic institutions of propertied society and the state. The earth would be shared communally, in a new spirit of harmony between man and man and between man and nature.

In the early years of the 19th century, this image of a new, free and stateless society was at best a distant vision, a humanistic ideal which revolutionaries described as communism or anarchism, and their opponents as utopia. As the one century passed into its successor, the advance of technology increasingly brought this vision into the realm of possibility. The ecological crisis of the late 20th century has now turned the possibility of its early decades into a dire necessity. Not only is humanity more prepared for the realization of this vision than at any time in history—a fact intuited by the tribalism of the youth culture—but upon its realization depends the very existence of humanity in the remaining years ahead.

Perhaps the most important message of Marx a century ago was the concept that humanity must develop the means of survival in order to live. Today, the development of a flexible, open-ended technology has reversed this concept completely. We stand on the brink of a post-scarcity society, a society that can finally remove material want and domination from the human condition. Perhaps the most important message of ecology is the concept that man must master the conditions of life in order to survive.

During the May-June uprising of 1968, the French students sensed the new equation in human affairs when they inscribed the demand: "Be realistic! Do the impossible!" To this demand, the young Americans who face the next century can add the more solemn injunction: "If we don't do the impossible, we shall be faced with the unthinkable."

Murray Bookchin is the author (under the name Lewis Herber) of Crisis in Our Cities *(Prentice-Hall, 1965, $5.65). He is a regular contributor to Anarchos magazine, specializing in the problems of man and the environment.*

Catch 24,400

(or, Plutonium Is My Favorite Element)

Roger Rapoport

There was a familiar ring to the fire alarm that sounded at 2:29 p.m. on May 11, 1969 at the Atomic Energy Commission (AEC) Rocky Flats plant, 16 miles upwind of central Denver. It signaled the latest in a series of over 200 fires that have occurred since the plant opened in 1953. But to hear the AEC tell it, Rocky Flats, which has the dangerous assignment of fabricating plutonium into nuclear triggers for hydrogen bombs and warheads, has built up an enviable safety record. Denverites who expressed concern about this latest accident were given a soothing, if somewhat evasive, official reply: "Rocky Flats ranks first in AEC facilities for safety and holds the fourth best all-time mark in American industry—2122 consecutive days (24,295,542 man-hours) without a disabling injury."

But all the press releases and National Safety Council plaques in Colorado didn't prevent plutonium from igniting spontaneously in the main production area on May 11. The flames leapt up inside the maze of glove boxes where plutonium is fabricated into parts for nuclear weapons. Tons of cellulose laminate shielding in the glove boxes fed the blaze, and it was nearly three hours before firemen brought the fire under control.

Days later Dow Chemical Co., which operates the plant for the AEC, reported that the fire had done $45 million worth of damage and burned $20 million worth of plutonium, enough to build about

77 Nagasaki-size atom bombs. But Dow and the AEC reassured increasingly nervous Colorado residents that no radiation had escaped from the safeguarded and specially constructed plant. Brandishing data compiled by the Colorado Department of Public Health and the U.S. Public Health Service, AEC spokesmen declared: "No appreciable amount of plutonium escaped from the building and no offsite contamination resulted from the fire."

This was supposed to be the last word. But for the over one million residents of Denver, it was the beginning of membership in the official AEC fairyland where accidents are infrequent, casualties unusual, pollution a forbidden word, and the gravestones carefully hidden from public view.

Since 1944 there have been 142 recorded atomic science fatalities, and cautious public health officials predict another 400 to 900 victims within the next 20 years. The conservatism in this estimate is clear when the facts are considered. In western towns, for instance, hundreds of thousands of tons of radioactive uranium mill wastes have been used as fill for construction sites and the radiation levels in some of the houses built on top of this waste are so high that residents are now being evacuated. AEC-sanctioned nuclear enterprises have contaminated the Colorado River, Lake Mead and the Great Salt Lake with radium; they have dumped radio-iodine into the Columbia River and released fission gases in Puerto Rico. They have seriously elevated iodine 131 levels in Utah milk and killed off deer and fish near Buffalo. And now two top experts predict that what the AEC regards as "allowable levels of radiation" could lead to as many as 32,000 extra cancer victims a year.

There are many reasons for this criminal irresponsibility. Most obvious is the fact that the AEC and its allies in industry have totalitarianized their hold over nuclear power. They probably have more freedom to pollute than any other power structure in the country. The AEC finances, licenses, regulates and polices itself. Other governmental agencies involved in the sampling or monitoring of radiation pollution are often forced to rely on inadequate AEC data, or are themselves funded (and controlled) by the AEC. Consultants for the atomic energy industry who work under AEC research grants crop up time and again as prime congressional witnesses proclaiming radiation is virtually harmless if kept below

Photograph by Carl Iwaski

the so-called "safe-threshold." And although atomic power reactors
are so dangerous that insurance companies will not cover them (the
public, through Congress, pays for $500 million worth of insurance
on each plant), when a state agency tries to set tough radiation
standards for proposed nuclear power plants in its area, it is immediately sued by the AEC.

Not only does the AEC control the scientific talent involved in
atomic power, it also determines which information about its activities reaches the public. It covers up mistakes with national security
blankets, and suppresses reports, scientists and employees critical
of its failures. Most Americans believe that there is no such thing as
radiation pollution. In fact, many of the new environmentalists are
little more than vaguely aware of this, the ultimate pollution. Look
at the official Handbook for the Environmental Teach-In: more
than 50 articles, over 360 pages, and not a single study of radiation
hazards.

A catalogue of the environmental crises we face is dangerously
incomplete without inclusion of the AEC and radiation pollution.
Atomic energy, in fact, is the conservation issue stripped bare of the
premature optimism some people now feel about our ability to stop

ecological damage. In the closed society that the AEC rules with an iron hand, there is no pretense of outside control.

Under the AEC's system of self-scrutiny, nuclear installations are free to contaminate both their workers and the public. The experience at Rocky Flats makes this clear. During the years the Colorado nuclear weapons production complex was being hailed as the safest of AEC plants, many workers there were being overexposed to plutonium. Plant officials refuse to say how many have died of cancer, but medical journal articles written by scientists employed at Rocky Flats admit that 325 workmen have been contaminated by radiation over the years. Between June 14, 1957 and October 28, 1958, there were 24 explosions, fires, plutonium spills and contamination incidents at the plant. According to congressional testimony, radioactive contamination has been found in the cafeteria, drinking fountains, sinks, laundered caps, shoes, drums, flasks, carts, lifts and saws—all these in the supposedly "cold" (non-radioactive) areas of the plant.

As in the case of the Santa Barbara oil disaster, technology to deal with accidents is almost non-existent. The AEC's solutions to the pollution it creates are almost pathetically inept. In 1968, for instance, a quantity of oil that had been contaminated by plutonium was scooped up, placed in a drum and trucked off from Rocky Flats to the official AEC burial grounds. En route, however, the drum began to leak, contaminating over a mile of highway. The AEC's solution was to repave the road. Unfortunately, plutonium's half-life of 24,400 years is a good deal longer than the full-life of asphalt, and many years from now, when the roadbed wears away, the hot plutonium will be exposed, to contaminate unborn generations.

After the May 11 fire, local scientists affiliated with the Colorado Committee for Environmental Information (CCEI) began to be skeptical of the Dow and AEC scientists. This independent group of college professors and privately-employed scientists asked the AEC to monitor Denver area soil for possible plutonium contamination from the fire.

In August 1969, Dow-AEC refused to make the plutonium soil samples. It explained to the CCEI that technical difficulties would make such a study inconclusive. So in the fall the CCEI's Dr. Edward Martell, a nuclear chemist with the National Center for

Atmospheric Research in Boulder, began conducting his own soil samples for plutonium. This former Pentagon specialist in nuclear weapons testing concluded his work in December 1969 and announced that highly lethal plutonium oxide from Rocky Flats had definitely spread out into metropolitan Denver during the May 11 holocaust. Martell found the highest plutonium contamination in areas east and southeast of the plant toward the Denver suburbs of Broomfield, Westminster and Arvada. High levels of plutonium were also found in Great Western Reservoir, part of the Broomfield water supply. The contamination of Denver ranged from 10 to 200 times higher than plutonium fallout deposited by all atomic bomb testing. And it was nearly 1000 times higher than the amount plant spokesmen said was being emitted.

The AEC and Dow sprang into action to try to counter Martell's facts. Bearing a cloak-and-dagger air, this counter-offensive began in early December when General Edward B. Giller, assistant AEC general manager for military application, learned that Martell was making independent soil samples and ordered the Rocky Flats staff to initiate similar work. Stanley Hammond, a chemist at Rocky Flats, even contacted Martell and asked for technical advice on how to make good soil samples for plutonium. Martell not only told him how to do it but sent some of his own soil samples over to Rocky Flats. The AEC study essentially corroborated Martell's data. As General Giller puts it: "So far we find his results are accurate, we don't disagree with his new data. As far as measurements, sampling techniques and knowledge of science we think Martell is a very competent scientist. Of course we question his interpretation of the new information. While it is true that some plutonium is escaping from the plant we don't believe it presents a significant health hazard to Denver." The AEC elaborated in a later press release: "Rocky Flats... has released trace amounts of plutonium.... However, these quantities have never shown a level of radioactivity in excess of the natural background radiation."

Background radiation is a favorite AEC game. Because the plutonium oxide particles from Rocky Flats emit dangerous alpha radiation, the agency tries to compare them with naturally occurring (background) particles that also emit alpha radiation. Dr.

Arthur R. Tamplin, an expert on the physiological effects of radiation and one of the few independent AEC scientists who have dared publicly to question the organization's dangerous nuclear mythology, explains what this means for Denver: "The Martell study shows about one trillion pure plutonium oxide particles [plutonium oxidizes in a fire] have escaped from Rocky Flats.These are very hot particles. You may only have to inhale 300 of them to double your risk of lung cancer. Inhaled plutonium oxide produces very intense alpha radiation dosage to lung tissue, thousands of times higher than the intensity for radioactive fallout particles and millions of times more intense than the dose from natural alpha radioactivity. An inhaled plutonium oxide particle stays in your lungs for an average of two years, emitting radiation that can destroy lung tissue. If the plutonium from the May 11 fire is being redistributed as Martell suggests, then it could increase the lung cancer rate for Denver by as much as 10 per cent. This could lead to as many as 2000 additional lung cancers in Denver."

Although Dr. Martell has already found a terrifying quantity of plutonium in Denver, he believes far more remains to be discovered. The Boulder scientist based his report on about 90 soil samples but believes hundreds more are necessary for a comprehensive insight into the extent of the contamination. He has urged that the federal government, independent of the AEC, launch a comprehensive soil sampling program in the Denver area.

Both federal and state agencies finally heeded Martell's call for a review of Rocky Flats, but their studies are neither comprehensive nor independent. President Nixon's top scientific advisory group, the Office of Science and Technology (OST), says it is now making an "independent analysis" of Rocky Flats contamination. Two AEC scientists from the agency's health and safety laboratory in New York have been taking 25 soil samples from sites in and around the plant. Results of these samples will be submitted to Dr. Hubert Heffner, deputy director of the OST, who says, "We have been assured [by the AEC] that this will be a comprehensive [sampling] program." Dr. Heffner plans to compare the AEC data with Martell's report and decide who is "more nearly right" in his measurements of contamination. While stating that he will not judge the case until all the data is in, Dr. Heffner declares, "My supposition is that the health consequences created by the plant are not severe."

A second independent study of Rocky Flats contamination is being conducted by the Colorado State Department of Health. The agency collected soil samples at 25 locations around Rocky Flats and sent them to the U.S. Public Health Service (USPHS) Southwestern Radiological Health Laboratory for analysis. The Las Vegas-based lab monitors the AEC's Nevada test site and is funded by the AEC.

Rocky Flats is not an isolated example of AEC totalitarianism. There has been bad news before, and it is always euphemized by AEC publicists capable of first-rate fiction. In the official agency booklet "USAEC—What It Is, What It Does," for example, it is claimed that, "The AEC has an impressive safety record. For example, since the beginning of the atomic energy program in 1942 there have been only seven deaths from nuclear causes among atomic energy workers in the United States." But U.S. Public Health Service studies show that 142 uranium miners have already died because of radiation overdoses ranging as much as 500 times over the safe level. And Charles C. Johnson, Jr., head of the U.S. Consumer Protection and Environmental Health Service, says, "Of the 6000 men who have been uranium miners, an estimated 600 to 1100 will die of lung cancer within the next 20 years because of radiation exposure on the job."

AEC negligence has spread the hazards of uranium mines into homes in western mill towns, allowing more than 300,000 tons of uranium mill tailings (which emit the same radon gas that has led to high incidence of lung cancer in uranium mines) to be used as construction fill in little towns like Grand Junction, Colorado. And about 60 miles northeast of Grand Junction the AEC is showcasing Project Rulison, one of its latest schemes for the peaceful use of atomic energy. In September 1969, the AEC detonated a 40-kiloton undergound nuclear explosion to free natural gas deposits. But now Project Rulison is a topic of debate among Colorado citizens because when the gas is flared, tritium and other radionuclides pollute the air. However, the AEC and its ally in the project, Austral Oil Co., have even more grandiose plans: they want to dilute the radioactive gas that was freed (but contaminated) by the blast by mixing it with uncontaminated gas; then they want to pump it into customers' homes.

The citizens around Rulison have gone into court to stop radiation pollution in their area. But even if the AEC should lose this battle, it still has the wider war to think of. For it is hoping to electrify homes and businesses with nuclear power. At the moment, about 75 American atomic power plants are planned or under construction. It is these nuclear power plants that comprise the largest hazard of radiation for the future. The 15 plants already built don't give much cause for optimism, since those in Michigan, New Jersey and Minneapolis are currently shut down due to malfunction. As far back as 1957, one of the AEC's own studies suggested that a reactor built 30 miles from the nearest city could kill 3400 people, injure 43,000 and cause $7 billion damage in a bad accident.

The AEC has a flock of experts devoted to studying radiation hazards. One of them is Dr. Wright Langham, a ranking AEC plutonium expert at Los Alamos, New Mexico. When American bombers accidentally dropped nuclear weapons on Palomares, Spain, it was Dr. Langham who rushed in to monitor plutonium contamination; he was subsequently awarded the Pentagon's Distinguished Service Medal in 1967 for his work. In a paper written for the Department of Health, Education and Welfare in 1968 on "The Problem of Large Area Plutonium Contamination," Dr. Langham says, "Plutonium is my favorite element. . . . The reputation of plutonium as a toxic material perhaps has contributed more than any other thing to my being supported in the modest though comfortable manner to which I have grown accustomed."

Scientists who formulate radiation protection standards say that safety is not the only consideration. For example, the International Commission on Radiological Protection reported: "At the present time, risk [health] considerations can at best play only a very general role in specific recommendations . . . and operational and administrative convenience must of necessity be of equal importance."

Despite the pressures to conform, two experts have started a crusade to stop the agency's radiation pollution. Charging that currently allowable radiation pollution could cause as many as 32,000 extra cancer deaths each year, they are calling for a ten-fold reduction in present radiation exposure limits.

The insurgent scientists, Drs. John Gofman and Arthur Tamplin of the Biomedical Division of the AEC's Lawrence Radiation Lab at Livermore, are among the nation's leading experts on the medical effects of radiation. Both Gofman and Tamplin have had a continuing interest in radiation dangers throughout their professional lives, but Gofman's concern was hard-earned and dates back to 1941 when he was a Berkeley graduate student studying under then Assistant Professor of Chemistry Glenn Seaborg.

Gofman and Seaborg co-discovered uranium 233 and the young student was assigned to demonstrate that U233 was fissionable with neutrons. Such evidence would open up the world's thorium supply as a vast new source of atomic energy. Gofman was to bombard the virgin isotope with a one-gram radium-beryllium neutron source. A gram of radium-beryllium is deadly stuff, and is moved about inside lead containers. To protect himself, Gofman went to work building a small conveyor that would transport the hot neutron source up to the U233 by remote control. But Professor Seaborg was impatient. One day he dropped by and chided Gofman for being overly concerned with safety. "The war will be over before you get any [fission] measurements this way," he said.

So Dr. Seaborg came up with a better idea. Gofman remembers being instructed to tie a rope to the radium-beryllium source and connect it to a big stick. Like a fisherman he could cast the hot neutron source across the room to the U233 where the fission test could be conducted. Seaborg left the room and Gofman did precisely what he was told. The experiment succeeded; U233 was fissionable. Seaborg went on to win the Nobel Prize and become chairman of the AEC; Gofman received a disastrous overdose of radiation, at least 100 times the permissible exposure level. So far, Gofman has fortunately not experienced any ill effects from the overexposure.

In 1963, Gofman, by then a Ph.D., M.D. and Professor of Medical Physics at Berkeley, was hired to head a new AEC biomedical lab at Livermore that would be devoted to studying radiation's effect on man and his environment. The lab was established in part to quell growing public concern about nuclear fallout, but after the Nuclear Test Ban Treaty was signed, the concern diminished and financial support for the lab waned.

As head of the Livermore Biomedical Lab and an associate director of the Lawrence Radiation Lab, Gofman hired biophysicist Tamplin. The tall, soft-spoken scientist pioneered the standard technique for measuring nuclear test fallout patterns, and with Gofman began to question the conventional AEC wisdom. At various symposiums the two men pointed out that AEC pet projects like nuclear excavation pose a grave health risk to the public. They also countered the official AEC theory of "acceptable levels of radiation" with the linear theory of radiation exposure which says that any radiation, no matter how slight, poses risks.

Indirectly, Gofman and Tamplin's crusade received a slight lift in early 1969 from University of Pittsburgh scientist Ernest Sternglass. In a widely quoted report, Sternglass charged that nuclear test fallout has caused 400,000 prenatal and infant mortalities. The AEC immediately asked Tamplin and several of his colleagues to do a critique of Sternglass' report. Tamplin agreed and presented a paper before an AEC Livermore symposium in April 1969 that declared Sternglass had overestimated the effects of fallout. Tamplin calculated that the fallout had caused only 4000 infant and prenatal mortalities, just one per cent of Sternglass' figure.

Tamplin proceeded to write up his report as an AEC technical paper. In August 1969 Tamplin's boss, Dr. John Totter, head of the AEC's Division of Biology and Medicine, tried to persuade Tamplin to delete a section from the paper. In a phone call on August 13, Totter and Spofford English, an assistant AEC general manager, tried to persuade Tamplin to criticize Sternglass but delete his risk estimate of 4000 infant and prenatal mortalities. Even though this was a mere fraction of the Sternglass estimate, the AEC executives did not want to lend any credence whatsoever to the Pittsburgh scientist's report. When Tamplin refused to accede to the telephone pressures from Washington, Totter wrote two letters reiterating his demand.

Tamplin ignored his AEC superiors and published the complete paper as a technical document. As AEC pressure on them built up, Gofman and Tamplin decided to fight back. In a San

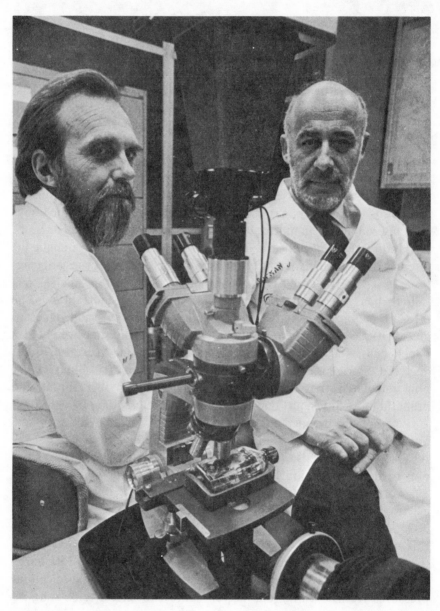

Photograph by Baron Wolman
Francisco speech in late October 1969, the two scientists publicly announced their call for a ten-fold cut in allowable radiation levels. Then in mid-November they reiterated their demand before the

U.S. Senate Public Works Subcommittee on Air and Water Pollution.

In December the AEC staff in Washington issued a nine-page critique of the California scientists' call for tougher radiation standards, and said there was nothing new in the Gofman-Tamplin paper, that the data was inconclusive and the report should have been published in a respectable, refereed scientific journal before it was released to Congress (this is the line the AEC has used unsuccessfully to try to persuade Tamplin to delete his risk estimate in the Sternglass critique). On this basis the AEC concluded there was no need for an official review of radiation protection standards.

But the Federal Radiation Council, which sets the nation's radiation protection standards, disagreed with the AEC. On January 28, 1970 the Council revealed that it was initiating an unprecedented review of radiation standards, as called for by Gofman and Tamplin. Instead of honoring Gofman and Tamplin, however, the scientific establishment snubbed them. On January 30, 1970 Phillip Abelson, editor of influential Science magazine, co-discoverer of neptunium and a charter member of the nuclear power fan club, rejected a Gofman-Tamplin paper on the need for tighter radiation standards. Then in early February, Science published a three-page critique of the Gofman-Tamplin work.

Thus we see what is required to get the nuclear power structure finally dragged into position for a bit of public scrutiny. But there is no cause for immediate optimism. Those like Gofman and Tamplin fighting within the scientific establishment, and those on the outside who believe the AEC can no longer be allowed to play judge, jury and nuclear hangman, face a long, long fight. The totalitarian polluter, despite all the adverse publicity, is still far more powerful than public opinion.

If you have any doubts about how these nabobs of nuclear power work, you should check out the current scene in Denver. While a few independent scientists wait on the fringes of the disaster to count extra lung cancers produced by the plutonium catastrophe at Rocky Flats, the AEC is on the scene with millions to spend on cleanup and publicity, piping in Muzak for the men scraping plutonium off the scorched floors and reminding all that the plant is a bulwark of national defense. Over 3000 employees are glad to have their jobs and some of them write letters to local newspapers suggesting all the talk about plutonium contamination in Denver is actually a Bolshevik scare tactic. Press releases handed out by Dow Chemical's public relations man Mike Carroll (a former FBI agent) try to soothe the public. Meanwhile, the security system (the AEC spent over $7 million for security investigations on its employees during 1969) is used to intimidate malcontents. After a newspaper article quoted a Rocky Flats worker complaining that he had leukemia and could not get workmen's compensation from the AEC, for instance, meetings were called throughout the plant. Management spokesmen castigated the man for talking to the press, and the plant manager wrote a letter to the editor noting that the workman's brother also had cancer, a fact that made it all a problem of heredity.

Its $45 million cleanup operation continues, and the AEC is also spending another $75 million to double Rocky Flats production facilities. There is one thing that is clear: there will surely be a fire next time. And another after that, and still others. There are only two ways for it to end: Either the AEC's power is shut off, or the Rocky Flats area becomes a plutonium mine.

Roger Rapoport is a free-lance journalist and co-author with L. J. Kirshbaum of Is the Library Burning? *(Random House, 1969, $4.95).*

Science and the
Gross National Pollution

George M. Woodwell

The world's fisheries are in danger. This year we lost the California mackerel catch. Last year it was the magnificently productive Coho salmon of Lake Michigan. Both fish were banned from interstate commerce because of DDT residues. If experience with the Coho salmon and other fish applies, we can expect the mackerel gradually to disappear, its young poisoned. Other fish will follow. This loss is especially significant because it indicates that the ocean is contaminated to the point that human food supplies are being reduced. But even more disturbing is the continued failure of American science to address itself to such problems clearly and effectively.

For a culture that is brutalized daily by casual brushes with war, it is perhaps unreasonable to expect a general outpouring of grief over one more crisis in the existence of a species of fish. But how can it be that the American scientific establishment, whose ingenuity and technology appear often to be almost infinitely versatile, is fumbling with the crisis of the environment? Science should have been intensely concerned with the devastation of the earth long before conspicuous disasters and grass-roots protests made ecology fashionable. But scientists have not been leaders in the protest, and now they are conspicuously unprepared for the environmental crisis and often even antagonistic. To understand this failure is to probe the way that science has grown in the United States over the past two decades; it is also, as with other aspects of ecology, to wonder about the wisdom of the present course of this country's political and economic systems.

[II]

A testament to the seriousness of the environmental problems and the inability of science to provide ready solutions comes from a look at a recent Health, Education and Welfare report by a special commission—the so-called "Mrak Commission"—on the relationship between pesticides and human health. One of its most striking conclusions points to "the absurdity of the situation in which 200 million Americans are undergoing lifelong exposure [to pesticides], yet our knowledge of what is happening to them is at best fragmentary and for the most part indirect and inferential." Despite this admission, however, the report observes that "production and use of pesticides in the United States is expected to grow at an annual rate of approximately 15 per cent." This rate of growth means that pesticide production will double every five years or so and that the hazards that science is now recognizing (not to mention those that haven't yet been uncovered because researchers have been busy elsewhere) can be expected to be at least twice as serious by 1974. To be sure, the Mrak Commission calls for an end to the use of DDT and DDD within two years, and it makes appropriate gestures to the possibilities for control of pests without using persistent pesticides. But nowhere does it challenge the wisdom of allowing production of these poisons to double every five years over the foreseeable future. Nor does it provide any appraisal of the future impact of this massive chemical assault on the living systems of the earth, or even recommend an expansion of research and regulatory activities appropriate to such a deadly growth rate. While a growth of 15 per cent is attractive in a portfolio of stocks, it is very difficult to maintain a highly integrated, complex social system that dumps poison at that rate into its own environment.

Pesticides are obviously no longer simply a national problem involving 200 million Americans. They are now a world problem. Recent studies with my colleagues at Brookhaven National Laboratory, and studies by others elsewhere, suggest that most of the DDT produced in the world has been held at one time or another as vapor in the atmosphere, is accumulating in the oceans and is having a catastrophic effect on the earth's biota. It has, in fact, become almost commonplace to point out that lakes and streams are being seriously degraded, bird populations reduced and in some cases eliminated, and oceanic fisheries jeopardized. The broad pattern is very clear. DDT and similar poisons are worldwide pollutants, products of Western technology that are rapidly transforming the ecosystems of the planet—from the complex communities that have built the biosphere and have supported oceanic fisheries and man, to the simplified biota of cesspools such as Lake Erie. How far can we go in reducing the earth's biota this way and still support large human populations?

The pesticides problem is of course not the only worldwide pollution scientists have handled poorly. It happens to be one of the most important and best known. Others are now appearing with terrifying regularity. Take for example the so-called "PCB," toxic polychlorinated phenyl compounds that appear to have a distribution similar to that of DDT. They are used in large quantities in various industries, later to vaporize and circulate freely throughout the biosphere. How much of these compounds there is now circulating is not known, nor are their effects on the biota known, although PCB's are certainly accumulated in living systems and are toxic to many kinds of organisms. And how many other toxic organic compounds are circulating in biologically significant quantities worldwide?

To these questions we must add the questions raised by combustion of gasoline containing 2.4 grams of lead per gallon; fossil fuels containing sulphur; the widespread use of mercuric compounds as fungicides and as anti-fouling compounds; wastes from chemical milling; and a host of other toxic inorganic substances. We must also add the broader scale of "toxic" effects due to changes in temperature of the earth caused by particulate matter in the atmosphere.

The broad pattern of changes caused by the accumulation of these toxic effects is simple enough, although not widely recognized. For an indication, we need only examine the areas around smelters such as those at Ducktown, Tennessee, and Sudbury, Ontario, where releases of oxides of sulphur have devastated the vegetation and animal life over many square miles. The same processes are now at work worldwide, involving not only sulphur, but a thousand other toxic substances. The losses are not simply robins, bluebirds, eagles, mackerel or trees, but the potential of the earth to support life, including man. And through all of this the scientist seems to have been more of a cause than a cure. How does this happen?

[III]

The current disarray and helplessness of science should not be surprising to anyone who has watched modern scientific trends in

this country, especially since the Cold War. Science has grown
during this period in two segments, one industrially supported and
the other supported by public funds. The overriding objectives of
industrially-supported science have always been stated candidly:
greater profits for industry. Profits are increased by spreading the
costs of waste treatment to as wide a group as possible, so that no
individual notices a significant effect and the costs need not be
borne by industry itself. Obviously, such a commitment leads much
more rapidly to a deteriorating environment than to spontaneous
solutions for that deterioration. Despite the increasing number of
advertisements by industry on the efficacy of their own research
into pollution, profits continue to come from spreading the costs of
waste treatment widely. It is fatuous to hope that any cures to the
environmental problem will arise in industry.

The objectives of publicly-supported science—that branch of
science potentially serving the broader public interest—on the other
hand, have been for the most part set by Congress and reflect the
country's official sense of what is important. Research money has
long been available for war—including chemical and biological
warfare and bomb-related physics—and for cancer-related chemistry and biology. And thus the tax-supported segment of science has
developed an elaborate technology and a corps of brilliant specialists in biochemistry and physics. A scattering of Nobel prizes and
other awards for accomplishments such as cracking the genetic code
has helped to fasten public attention on these brilliant scientists,
reinforcing the direction in which their research was going and
strengthening the trend they represented.

As the scale and influence of science increased through the late
'50's and early '60's, the attention of scientists themselves shifted
from the original "practical" ones of war, bombs and cancer to
"basic research," a phrase that usually meant more biochemistry
and more nuclear physics, although of a less pragmatic nature.
There was also a strong tendency to allow the scientists themselves
to determine where research money should go. It is hardly surprising that the aristocracy of science that grew under these circumstances to hold high posts in academia and government was dominated by biochemists and even more by physical scientists. Nor is it
surprising that the bias of the new elite of science was reflected in

textbooks and school curricula, thus influencing future generations of scientists.

Throughout all this, environment as a subject was generally scorned within the scientific aristocracy. Environmental problems that were serious enough were thought amenable to quick technological cures. But now, suddenly after decades of neglect, the environment is in crisis. When wise and massive action in science and government is demanded, the American man of science is stumbling. He is stumbling in part because he was led by the availability of money to participate in building into society a large intellectual deficit—a deficit of research, of knowledge, of public understanding of the structure and function of environment, and a deficit of administrators experienced with environmental problems. He is stumbling also because he fears he is obsolete, too specialized, too vulnerable to the changing winds of the politics of science as determined by the needs of industry and government. In uncertainty, he is rushing to re-examine himself, the problem and his tools; but there is danger that he will simply try to rename his work "environmental" and set to work applying corn plasters to the cancer.

The exploiters of the environment have much to gain by subtly opposing further knowledge on subjects that might inhibit their rights as exploiters. Thus they create doubt and force compromise by questioning the accuracy, integrity and objectivity of science when it fails to support them.

Ultimately there must come recognition that the environmental crisis is a confrontation between man and nature; between human systems whose influence is now global, and the natural ecosystems that have built and maintain the biosphere as a place suitable for life. How much DDT, how many pesticides, how much fossil fuel, lead, sulphur and particulate matter can we spew into the atmosphere? How do we make the transition from unrestrained growth to limited growth, even to stability in many segments of national economies—a stability dictated by the dimensions of the earth? There are powerful forces aligned against finding a rational approach to this transition. Growth has many advocates; restraint has few.

The immediate crisis requires specific new knowledge of environment to reconcile the confrontation between man and nature.

Solutions, if there are any to be found, will deal with the transition from growth to stability and will have far-reaching political and social implications. What does stability mean for society? For technology? Does it mean no change at all? Or does it not mean that limits must be defined: the limits of the biosphere, the oceans, continents, estuaries, cities, and of the agricultural and natural ecosystems that support them; the limits of power development, of water. And it must mean also that the limits of man are to be explored, the limits of social and political systems. And deliberate attempts made to keep human activities small enough to be within these limits to avoid worldwide disasters. These are new objectives for science and for government.

The hope—and it is as yet a very dim one—is that the nations which can afford it will, perhaps propelled by their young people, very soon recognize that they must address themselves in a massive way to the overriding issue of whether or not complex human civilization is going to survive.

George M. Woodwell is senior ecologist at Brookhaven National Laboratory and a lecturer at Yale University.

The Making of a Pollution-Industrial Complex

Martin Gellen

In January of this year Coca-Cola Company announced its purchase of Aqua-Chem, a leading manufacturer of water treatment equipment and desalination systems. "The acquisition will permit Coca-Cola to enter the mainstream of environmental control systems," declared a spokesman for the company. Perhaps the people at Coke have seen the handwriting on the wall and realize that their livelihood depends on having clean water to make brown. But whatever the precise reasoning, the marriage of Coke and Aqua-Chem is just one among a rash of similar developments on Wall Street where pollution control has emerged as one of the hottest growth industries of the '70's. As Forbes Magazine put it in a recent cover story, "there's cash in all that trash."

Since the beginning of December 1969, despite a market engaged in a remarkably stubborn downward spiral, stock issues of companies with substantial interests in pollution control have made price advances of often better than 50 per cent. For instance, Research-Cottrell, Inc., the largest of the corporations devoted entirely to environmental systems, has quadrupled its sales in five years. For the pollution control industry as a whole, the average annual growth rate for the next five years is expected to climb to better than 20 per cent, which is almost three times that of most manufacturing groups.

Lester Krellenstein, an engineer and pollution control promoter for the brokerage firm of H. Hentz and Company, believes that President Nixon's appointment of a Council of Environmental Quality triggered the heavy buying. According to Krellenstein, "A great deal of money is going to be made in this business." Present estimates of the potential market start at $25 billion.

But of all the developments in the fledgling industry, by far the most instructive is the corporate integration of polluters and controllers. About two dozen pollution control companies are subsidiaries or divisions of the largest corporations and polluters in the United States. Represented among this latter group are Dow Chemical Co., Monsanto Chemical, W. R. Grace, DuPont, Merck, Nalco, Union Carbide, General Electric, Westinghouse, Combustion Engineering, Honeywell, Beckman Instruments, Alcoa, Universal Oil Products, North American Rockwell, and many others. Although these super-corporations currently make less in sales from pollution control than do smaller firms like Research-Cottrell and Wheelabrator, their superior access to capital, resources, markets, management skills and political power will invariably be translated into a superior competitive position as the ecology movement flowers and the control industry grows.

[II]

The pollution control industry is really an extension of both the technological capabilities and the marketing patterns of the capital goods sector of the economy. Most of the companies involved in pollution control are not only polluters themselves but are the same firms which supply the chemicals, machines, plant fuels and parts for even bigger polluters, such as General Motors, U.S. Steel, Boeing, Standard Oil, Philco-Ford, American Can Co. and Consolidated Edison. For many of these firms, pollution control is merely one aspect of a program of "environmental diversification," which is generally accompanied by heavy investment and aggressive acquisition programs.

Koppers, for instance, is an engineering and construction firm that designs municipal sewage plants as well as air and water purification systems. Among its many specialties in pollution abatement is the production of gas removal devices for electric utilities, steel plants, coke plants and foundries. At the same time, however, Koppers is one of the world's leading builders of steelmaking equipment and is responsible for designing over 25 per cent of all basic steelmaking facilities in the U.S., as well as half of the present domestic coke plants in operation. Thus it gets the business coming and going. Since 80 per cent of the coke plants in the nation will require modernization in the '70's, and the steel industry expects to increase its overall capacity by 50 per cent, Koppers can expect good profits designing the pollution control systems needed to curb the pollution caused by all the new coke ovens, steel furnaces and foundries which it will construct.

It is the chemical industry, however, that best illustrates the consequences of the incest between the pollution control business and the industrial polluters. First, the chemical industry is in the enviable position of reaping sizable profits by attempting to clean up rivers and lakes (at public expense) which they have profitably polluted in the first place. To facilitate this, practically every major chemical company in the U.S. has established a pollution abatement division or is in the process of doing so. Dow Chemical, for example, produces a wide variety of products and services for water pollution abatement, including measuring instruments, specialty treatment chemicals, and a special biological filter medium called SURF-PAC. The company designs, engineers, builds and services waste water treatment plants and is currently supervising municipal sewage plants in Cleveland and working on waste disposal problems for lumber companies in Pensacola, Florida, and West Nyack, New York. All of these projects are funded by the Federal Water Pollution Control Administration (FWPCA).

Thus, the chemical industry—which ranks second in production of polluted waste water and generates close to 50 per cent of the biological oxygen demand in industrial water before treatment—has, at the same time, established a dominant position in the water pollution control business.

A second consequence of placing the "control" of pollution in the hands of big business is that the official abatement levels will inevitably be set low enough to protect industry's power to pollute and therefore its ability to keep costs down and revenues high. According to a recent study by the FWPCA, if the chemical industry were to reduce its pollution of water to zero, the costs involved would amount to almost $2.7 billion per year. This would cut profits almost by half.

Fortunately for the chemical industry, the present abatement target is only 75 per cent reduction in water pollution through "secondary treatment" methods which will clean up the solids but leave the phosphates, nitrogen compounds and a host of other poisonous substances which secondary treatment can't possibly catch.

Of course, it is precisely the profit incentive as the criterion of what shall and shall not be produced that makes it impossible to stop the proliferation and profusion of poisons in even the most obvious places. Thus, the chemical industry has polluted the housewife's food package not only through the unintended absorption of pesticide residues, but also through innumerable colorings, additives (like the cyclamates) and preservatives designed to increase food purchases and consumption, in order to buoy up sagging sales curves. The package itself, which is a sales boosting device par excellence, can be both the most polluting and dangerous feature of all. As a piece de resistance the chemical industry produces the non-biodegradable plastic container, which comes in all sizes, shapes and colors, and, if made from polyvinyl plastic, like Dow's Saran-Wrap, can be deadly in the most literal sense of the word. When Saran-Wrap is accumulated as trash and burned, it produces phosgene gas—a poison gas used in World War I and currently stockpiled by the Department of Defense. Exposure for only a short duration to 50 parts of phosgene per million parts of air will cause death. The chemical industry currently makes approximately five billion pounds of polyvinyl plastic per year and output is expected to rise by seven per cent this year alone.

Another consequence of business control of cleaning up the environment is cost to the public. Most municipal water treatment plants in large urban areas are currently constructed to handle an excess capacity frequently 100 per cent greater than the volume of waste actually produced by their resident populations. Much of this surplus capacity is used by big business (especially the chemical industry) to dispose of its wastes. Although industries are charged for this use, it is the consumers and taxpayers, through federal grants and state bonds, who bear the cost of construction and maintenance of the treatment facilities. Thus the public pays the polluters to construct the treatment facilities necessitated by the polluters in the first place.

Thus pollution control, developed as a complementary industry, is a way to insure that the favorable balance between cost, sales and profits can be maintained and business can continue as usual—

indeed, better than usual, for pollution control means new investment outlets, new income and new profits; the more waste, the better. Pollution control as conceived by the pollution control industry is merely an extension of the same pattern of profit-seeking exploitation and market economics which is at the root of the environmental crisis itself.

[III]

The most salient fact about the crisis that now threatens to overwhelm us is that it is first and foremost a product of the so-called free-enterprise system. "American business," as Fortune admits, "since it organizes and channels a high proportion of the total action of this society, has been and still is deeply implicated in depredations against the environment." It is not technology per se, but the way technology is employed (its organization and channeling) that creates the problems. Take, for example, the automobile. What logic determined man's use, as his central mode of transportation, of a device which threw concrete highways across the plains, cut up the forests, poisoned the atmosphere, congested the cities and created the sprawling conurbations that have smothered the land? Was it safe? Computed as fatalities per mile, the death rate for cars is 25 times that for trains and 10 times that for planes. Was it efficient? A traffic study made in 1907 shows that horse-drawn vehicles in New York moved at an average speed of 11.5 miles per hour. Today, automobiles crawl at the average daytime rate of six miles per hour.

At the beginning of the '60's it was estimated that in a single day, motor vehicles burned about seven million gallons of gasoline and in the process produced enough carbon monoxide to pollute the air to a depth of 400 feet over an area of 681 square miles. One-third of the entire land area of Los Angeles (two-thirds of the downtown section) had been absorbed by cars and trucks and the facilities to service them. The area was so congested that plans were laid to spend another $7.5 billion over the next decade on highway construction. The highway program would cost $10,000 per family, while during the same period only $3090 per family would be spent in Los Angeles County for schools, hospitals, parks, water supply, recreation and all other facilities. And Los Angeles is no worse in this respect than other city or urban areas. New York is now spending $100 million per mile to construct a crosstown highway. But in the peak hours, 87.6 per cent of the people entering the central business district come by public transport (71 per cent by subway).

Is there any rationality in all this? There is. But it is a private rationality. The essence of the private property system is that social technology and production are privately or corporately organized and channeled through the market. Thus, in launching his new product, Henry Ford had only private costs to reckon (i.e., the costs to him in labor, materials, etc.). The individual consumer who bought the car had only to reckon his personal preferences versus the purchase price. The question of who would pay the costs of roads, of restructuring cities and organizing the flow of traffic, was taken care of by Ford, the rubber industry, the glass industry, the concrete industry and related interests getting together and twisting the arm of the government. They saw to it that the public would pay for solving the problems created by the new machine.

The costs of pollution are borne by our lungs and in individual cleaning bills; the costs of lack of safety are paid in individual hospital bills and individual deaths. Suppose Ford had been forced from the outset to reckon the social costs (at least the ones that could be quantified) and to put that in the price of his autos. At that price, people would have bought trains as their mass transportation, or more reasonably, they would have been forced to structure their cities and communities in a way which would have enabled them to walk to virtually all of the places necessary.

The problems created by the market system are thus like original sin: their implications keep spreading and diversifying. Now, when the demand for cars shows signs of being saturated, the market strategists get to work and—by changing models, manipulating consumers and planning the obsolescence of their product—generate the need for more and more cars, ad infinitum. The waste in resources is staggering (it has been estimated that style changes in autos alone cost $4 billion annually) and the increase in pollution incalculable.

The pollution control industry itself reflects this irrationality in production for profit. It, too, is a growth industry. It, too, depends for its existence on society's capacity to make waste. The production of steel, copper, aluminum, asbestos and beryllium components for air pollution systems and sewage plants will probably create more air pollution and kill more rivers. The waste involved in the production of all the specialty chemicals and biological agents needed for water treatment alone is staggering. Moreover, the waste in resources required to operate $100 billion worth of control systems will certainly not reduce the despoliation of the environment.

Instead of reorganizing the productive system for social ends, thereby eliminating the problem of waste production and distribution at its source, pollution control under business auspices amounts to no more than rationalizing and improving waste production by making it less ugly, less harmful, less objectionable, and more pleasant for everybody. The object of this kind of pollution control is to make pollution "functional" in society, to institutionalize it, to change it into a necessary and regular part of the everyday world. There is no more effective way to do that than to make it possible for a whole industry to make money out of it. To the military-industrial complex, we can now add an eco-pollution-industrial complex, with a vested interest in continuing economic growth and environmental malaise.

The philosophical justifications for this "solution" are already well developed. As President Nixon's science adviser, Dr. Lee A. DuBridge, puts it, "Let's face it—waste products are a fact of life we have to recognize. . . . Clearly, the U.S. will be producing more waste in the future—not less." The purpose of pollution control, DuBridge explains, is simply to "determine reasonable levels of pollution consistent with good health." Such a logic simultaneously justifies the political economy of waste, effectively de-politicizes the issues of the environment, and defines the problem of pollution in terms of technological solutions and bureaucratic directives. As such it is the normal logic of a society whose business, as Coolidge once said, is business.

[IV]

Following every failure of the business system in a major social area, the government has stepped in to create a new social-industrial complex, passing the costs of rehabilitation and correction on to the taxpaying public, and reserving the benefits for the corporations. Like the defense suppliers and the educational-man-power conglomerates, the pollution control industry now enjoys the good fortune of being legislated into success. Lavish profits will come from ready-made markets bolstered by special laws control-ling pollution levels of factories, special tax write-offs for the industrial buyers of abatement equipment, and plenty of R&D money for the pollution controllers themselves. As government outlays on abatement grow, so will the profits accruing to the pollu-tion control industry. With Uncle Sam posing as Mr. Clean, the crisis of the environment can't help being profitable.

Photograph by Alan Copeland/Photon West

At the National Executives Conference on Water Pollution Abatement, convened last fall by the Department of Interior in order to "bring the environmental programs of business and government into close alignment," John Gillis, president of Monsanto Chemical Co., led the business executives in calling for immediate federal financial aid in the form of quick tax write-offs and investment credits. The Tax Reform Bill passed by Congress early this winter answered the call. While abolishing the seven per cent investment credit, Congress instituted a special five-year amortization allowance for pollution control equipment, which will actually allow a lot of corporations somewhat larger tax deductions than did the investment credit. In addition, some 22 states also offer such subsidies for installation of pollution control equipment. California, for example, provides for a special five-year write-off, while Connecticut gives anti-polluters a five per cent tax credit.

With the prospects of rising R&D expenditures by the federal government, everyone is getting into the act. Anaconda and Alcoa have recently established environmental divisions. Esso Research has started a five-year planning study to determine the National Air Pollution Control Administration (NAPCA) needs in the area of nitrogen oxide emission control. The presence of aerospace corporations and other major defense contractors like Dow, G.E. and Westinghouse on the federal pollution control payroll is of course more than mere coincidence. Currently, the aerospace industry receives about 25 per cent of all the research contracts awarded by NAPCA. Aerojet-General, Avco Industries, Bendix Corporation and Litton Industries are some of the more prominent newcomers to the field. For Litton, Bendix and Aerojet-General, pollution control is a spin-off from their government-sponsored programs for development of biological weapons. Aerojet-General has also received over a million dollars in contracts from the Federal Water Pollution Control Administration for control of toxic agents in water supplies.

After riot control, pollution control is another area in which North American Rockwell, builder of Apollo and one of the country's biggest defense contractors, expects to make "important social contributions as well as profits," according to Robert T. Chambers, chairman of Envirotech, which is NAR's new pollution abatement subsidiary. Envirotech will market some of the measuring devices which NAR has developed through work for FWPCA, NAPCA, the Defense Department's chemical and biological warfare programs, and the space program. Just to keep it all in the family, President Nixon is reportedly planning to place the coordination of pollution control R&D programs under the aegis of the National Aeronautics and Space Administration instead of setting up a special agency for this purpose.

Nixon is also arranging to whip up a little business for investment bankers. As a part of Nixon's $10 billion program for municipal sewage plant construction, state and local governments will finance their $6 billion share of the deal through tax-exempt bonds. The President will also establish an Environmental Funding Authority to buy up any of the bonds which the locals can't sell. The EFA will probably handle a good number of them, since the municipal and state government bond markets are currently glutted. Its own funds would come from the sale of bonds at the even higher non-municipal rates. The Treasury Department (headed by banker David Kennedy) would make up the difference between the interest the EFA would receive on local bonds and what it would have to pay out on its own. In other words, the taxpayers would once again pay the bill.

Thus, pollution control programs illustrate the ways in which government promotes the welfare of business at the expense of the taxpaying public. The non-taxpaying poor will also suffer. It's all a matter of priorities. More federal spending for pollution control will mean less for the war on poverty. "Ultimately," pontificates the Wall Street Journal, "preservation of the environment may have to take absolute priority over social stability and welfare."

The crisis of the environment must be viewed in terms of a paradox central to modern society. The mobilization of the productive energies of society and the physical forces of nature for the purpose of accumulating profits or enhancing private power and privilege now conflicts directly with the universal dependence of men upon nature for the means of their common survival. A society whose principal ends and incentives are monetary and expansionist inevitably produces material and cultural impoverishment—in part precisely because of the abundance of profitable goods. To make an industry out of cleaning up the mess that industry itself makes is a logical extension of corporate capitalism. What is needed, however, is not an extension of what is already bad, but its transformation into something better.

Martin Gellen is an associate of the Bay Area Institute for Policy Studies and is presently doing organizing around environmental issues.

Santa Barbara: Oil in

the Velvet Playground

Harvey Molotch

Santa Barbara seems worlds apart both from the sprawling Los Angeles metropolis a hundred miles further south on the coast highway and from the avant-garde San Francisco Bay Area to the north. It has always been calm, clean and orderly. Of the city's 70,000 residents, a large number are upper and upper-middle class. They are people who have a wide choice of places in the world to live, but they have chosen Santa Barbara because of its ideal climate, gentle beauty and sophistication. Hard-rock Republicans, they vote for any GOP candidate who comes along, including Ronald Reagan and Max Rafferty, California's right-wing Superintendent of Public Education.

Under normal circumstances, Santa Barbarans are not the sort of people who are accustomed to experiencing stark threats to their survival, or arbitrary, contemptuous handling of their wishes. They are an unlikely group to be forced to confront brutal realities about how the "normal channels" in America can become hopelessly clogged and unresponsive. Yet this is exactly what happened when the Union Oil Company's well erupted in the Santa Barbara Channel last January, causing an unparalleled ecological disaster, the effects of which are still washing up on the local beaches.

In the ensuing months it became clear that more than petroleum had leaked out from Union Oil's drilling platform. Some basic truths about power in America had spilled out along with it. The oil disaster was more than simply another omen for an increasingly "accident-prone" civilization. Precisely because it was an accident —a sudden intrusion into an extremely orderly social process—it provided Santa Barbarans with sharp insights into the way our society is governed and into the power relationships that dictate its functions.

Across the political spectrum in Santa Barbara, the response has been much the same: fury. Some, including persons who never before had made a political move in their lives, were led from petition campaigns to the picket line and demonstrations, to the sit-down, and even to the sail-in. The position they finally came to occupy shows that radicalism is not, as experts like Bruno Bettelheim have implied, a subtle form of mental imbalance caused by rapid technological change or by the increasing impersonality of the modern world; radicals are not "immature," "undisciplined" or "anti-intellectual." Quite the contrary. They are persons who live in conditions where injustice is apparent, and who have access to more complete information about their plight than the average man, giving them a perspective that allows them to become angry in a socially meaningful way. In short, radicals are persons who make the most rational (and moral) response, given the social and political circumstances. Thus, as recent sociological studies have shown, radical movements like SDS draw their memberships disproportionately from the most intelligent and informed members of their constituent populations.

[OPTIMISTIC INDIGNATION: GOVERNMENT BY THE PEOPLE]

For over fifteen years, Santa Barbara's political leaders attempted to prevent the despoilation of their coastline by oil drilling in adjacent federal waters. Although they were unsuccessful in blocking the leasing of *federal* waters beyond the three-mile limit, they were able to establish a sanctuary within *state* waters (thus foregoing the extraordinary revenues which leases in such areas bring to adjacent localities). It was therefore a great irony that the one city which had voluntarily exchanged revenue for a pure environment should find itself faced, in January of 1969, with a massive eruption which was ultimately to cover the entire city coastline with a thick coat of crude oil. The air was soured for many hundreds of feet inland, and tourism—the traditional economic base of the region—was severely threatened. After ten days, the runaway well was brought under control, only to erupt again in February. This fissure was closed in March, but was followed by a sustained "seepage" of oil—a leakage which continues today to pollute the sea, the air and the famed local beaches. The oil companies had paid a record $603 million for their lease rights, and neither they nor the federal government bore any significant legal responsibility toward the localities which those lease rights might endanger.

The response of Santa Barbarans to this pollution of their near-perfect environment was immediate. A community organization called "GOO" (Get Oil Out!) was established under the leadership of a former state senator and a local corporate executive. GOO took a strong stand against any and all oil activity in the Channel and circulated a petition to that effect which eventually gained 110,000 signatures and was sent to President Nixon. The stodgy Santa Barbara News-Press (oldest daily newspaper in Southern California, its masthead proclaims) inaugurated a series of editorials, unique in their uncompromising stridency and indicative of the angry mood of the community. "The people of the Santa Barbara area can never be repaid for the hurt that has been done to them and their environment," said a front-page editorial. "They are angry—and this is not the time for them to lose their anger. This is the time for them to fight for action that will guarantee absolutely and permanently that there will be no recurrence of the nightmare of the last two weeks. . . ."

The same theme emerged in the hundreds of letters published by the News-Press in the weeks that followed and in the positions taken by virtually every local civic and government body. Rallies were held at the beach, and GOO petitions were circulated at local shopping centers and sent to sympathizers around the country. Local artists, playwrights, advertising men, retired executives and academic specialists from the local campus of the University of California executed special projects appropriate to their areas of expertise.

A GOO strategy emerged for an attack on two fronts. Local indignation, producing the petition to the President and thousands of letters to key members of Congress and the executive, would lead to appropriate legislation. Legal action against the oil companies

GOO! pickets on Santa Barbara wharf, among them John Schaff, painting contractor; Bud Bottorns, G. E. Tempo employee; Kenneth Miller [Ross McDonald] mys-
tery writer. Photograph courtesy of Sierra Club.

and the federal government would have the double effect of recoup-
ing some of the financial losses certain to be suffered by the local
tourist and fishing industries while at the same time serving notice
that drilling in the Channel would become a much less profitable
operation. Legislation to ban drilling was introduced by Senator
Alan Cranston in the U.S. Senate and Representative Charles
Teague in the House of Representatives. Joint suits for $1 billion in
damages were filed against the oil companies and the federal
government by the city and county of Santa Barbara (later joined
by the State of California).

All of these activities—petitions, rallies, court action and legislative lobbying—expressed their proponents' basic faith in "the
system." There was a muckraking tone to the Santa Barbara protest: the profit-mad executives of Union Oil were ruining the coastline, but once national and state leaders became aware of what was

going on and were provided with the "facts" of the case, justice would be done.

Indeed, there was good reason for hope. The quick and enthusiastic responses of the right-wing Teague and the liberal Cranston represented a consensus of men otherwise polar opposites in their political behavior. But from other important quarters there was silence. Santa Barbara's representatives in the state legislature either said nothing or (in later stages) offered only minimal support. Most disappointing of all to Santa Barbarans Governor Ronald Reagan withheld support for proposals which would end the drilling.

As subsequent events unfolded, the seemingly inexplicable silence of most of the democratically-elected representatives began to fall into place as part of a more general pattern. Santa Barbarans began to see American democracy as a very complicated affair—not simply a system in which governmental officials carry out the desires of their constituents once those desires become known. Instead, increasing recognition came to be given to the "all-powerful Oil lobby"; to legislators "in the pockets of Oil"; to academicians "bought" by Oil and to regulatory agencies that lobby for those they are supposed to regulate. In other words, Santa Barbarans became increasingly ideological, increasingly sociological and, in the words of some observers, increasingly "radical." Writing from his lodgings in the Santa Barbara Biltmore, the city's most exclusive residence hotel, an irate citizen penned these words in a letter published in the local paper: "We the People can protest and protest and it means nothing because the industrial and military junta are the country. They tell us, the People, what is good for the oil companies is good for the People. To that I say, Like Hell! ... Profit is their language and the proof of all this is their history."

[DISILLUSIONMENT: GOVERNMENT BY OIL]

From the start, Secretary of Interior Walter Hickel was regarded with suspicion, and his publicized associations with Alaskan oil interests did little to improve his image in Santa Barbara. When he called a halt to drilling immediately after the initial eruption, some Santa Barbarans began to believe that he would back them up. But even the most optimistic were quite soon forced to recognize that government policy would indeed confirm their worst fears. For, only one day later, Secretary Hickel ordered a resumption of drilling and production—even as the oil continued to gush into the Channel.

Oil staining Santa Barbara beach. Photograph courtesy of Sierra Club

Within 48 hours Hickel reversed his position and ordered another halt to the drilling. But this time his action was seen as a direct response to the massive nationwide media play then being given to the Santa Barbara plight and to the citizens' mass outcry just then beginning to reach Washington. Santa Barbarans were further disenchanted with Hickel and the executive branch both because the Interior Department failed to back any legislation to halt drilling and because it consistently attempted to downplay the entire affair—minimizing the extent of the damages and hinting at possible "compromises" which were seen locally as near-total capitulation to the oil companies.

One question on which government officials systematically erred on the side of Oil was that of the *volume* of oil spilling into the Channel. The U.S. Geological Survey (administered by the Department of the Interior), when queried by reporters, produced estimates which Santa Barbarans could only view as incredible. Located in Santa Barbara is a technological establishment among the most sophisticated in the country—the General Research Corporation, a research and development firm with experience in marine technology. Several officials of the corporation made their own study of the oil outflow and announced findings of pollution volume at a minimum of *ten-fold* that of the government's estimate. The methods which General Research used to prepare its estimates were made public. The Geological Survey and the oil interests, however, continued to blithely issue their own lower figures, refusing to provide any substantiating arguments.

Another point of contention was the effect of the oil on the beaches. The oil companies, through various public relations officials, constantly minimized the actual amount of damage and maximized the effect of Union Oil's cleanup activities; and the Department of the Interior seemed determined to support Union Oil's claims. Thus Hickel referred at a press conference to the "recent" oil spill, providing the impression that the oil spill was over at a time when freshly erupting oil was continuing to stain local beaches. When President Nixon appeared locally to "inspect" the damage to beaches, Interior arranged for him to land his helicopter on a city beach which had been thoroughly cleaned in the days just before, thus sparing him a close-up of much of the rest of the county shoreline, which continued to be covered with a thick coat of crude oil. (The beach visited by Nixon has been oil-stained on many occasions subsequent to the President's departure.) Secret servicemen kept the placards and shouts of several hundred demonstrators at a safe distance from the President.

The damage to the "ecological chain," while still of unknown proportions, was treated in a similarly deceptive way. A great many

Photograph by Dick Smith

birds died from oil which they had ingested while trying to preen their oil-soaked feathers—a process Santa Barbarans saw in abundant examples. In what local and national authorities called a hopeless task, two bird-cleaning centers were established (with help from oil company money) to cleanse feathers and otherwise minister to injured wildfowl. Spokesmen from both Oil and the federal government then adopted these centers as sources of "data" on the extent of damage to the bird life. Thus, the number of birds killed by oil pollution was computed on the basis of the number of fatalities at the wildfowl centers. It was a preposterous method and was recognized as such. Clearly, the dying birds in the area were provided with inefficient means of propelling themselves to these designated centers.

At least those birds in the hands of local ornithologists could be confirmed as dead, and this fact could not be disputed by either Oil or Interior. This was not so, however, with species whose corpses are more difficult to produce on command. Several official observers at the Channel Islands, a national wildlife preserve containing one of the country's largest colonies of sea animals, reported sighting unusually large numbers of dead sea lion pups on the oil-stained shores of one of the islands. Statement and counter-statement followed, with Oil's defenders (including the Department of the Navy) arguing that the animals were not dead at all, but only appeared inert because they were sleeping. In a similar case, the dramatic beaching in Northern California of an unusually large number of dead whales—whales which had just completed their migration through the Santa Barbara Channel—was acknowledged, but held not to be caused by oil pollution.

In the end, it was not simply the Interior Department, its U.S. Geological Survey and the President who either supported or tacitly accepted Oil's public relations tactics. The regulatory agencies at both national and state levels, by action, inaction and implication, effectively defended Oil at virtually every turn. In a letter to complaining citizens, for instance, N. B. Livermore Jr. of the Resources Agency of California referred to the continuing oil spill as "minor seepage" with "no major long term effect on the marine ecology." The letter adopted the perspective of Interior and Oil, even though the state was in no way being held culpable for the spill. This tendency was so blatant that it led the State Deputy Attorney General, Charles O'Brien, to charge the state conservation boards with "industry domination." Thomas Gaines, a Union Oil executive, actually sits on the state agency board most directly connected with the control of pollution in Channel waters.

Understandably enough, Secretary Hickel's announcement that the Interior Department was generating new "tough" regulations to control off-shore drilling was met with considerable skepticism. The Santa Barbara County Board of Supervisors was invited to "review" these new regulations and refused to do so in the belief that such participation would be used to provide a false impression of democratic responsiveness.

In previous years when they were fighting against the leasing of the Channel, the Supervisors had been assured of technological safeguards; now, as the emergency continued, they could witness for themselves the absence of any method for ending the leakage in the Channel. They also had heard the testimony of Donald Solanas, a regional supervisor of Interior's U.S. Geological Survey, who said about the Union platform eruption: "I could have had an engineer on that platform 24 hours a day, seven days a week and he couldn't have prevented the accident." His explanation of the cause of the "accident"? "Mother earth broke down on us." Given these facts,

Santa Barbarans saw Interior's proposed regulations—and the invitation to the County to participate in making them—as only a ruse to preface a resumption of drilling.

Their suspicions were confirmed when the Interior Department announced a selective resumption of drilling "to relieve pressures." The new "tough" regulations were themselves seriously flawed by the fact that most of their provisions specified measures (such as buoyant booms around platforms, use of chemical dispersants, etc.) which had proven almost totally useless in the current emergency.

The new regulations did specify that oil companies would henceforth be financially responsible for damages resulting from pollution mishaps. Several of the oil companies have now entered suit (supported by the ACLU) against the federal government, complaining that the arbitrary changing of lease conditions deprives them of rights of due process

Irritations with Interior were paralleled by frustrations encountered in dealing with the congressional committee which had the responsibility of holding hearings on ameliorative legislation. A delegation of Santa Barbarans was scheduled to testify in Washington on the Cranston bill to ban drilling. From the questions which congressmen asked them, and the manner in which they were "handled," the delegates could only conclude that the committee was "in the pockets of Oil." As one of the returning delegates put it, the presentation bespoke of "total futility."

At this writing, six months after their introduction, both the Cranston and Teague bills, though significantly softened, lie buried in committee with little prospect of surfacing.

[DISILLUSIONMENT: POWER IS KNOWLEDGE]

The American dream is a dream of progress, of the efficacy of know-how and technology; science is seen as both servant and savior. From the start, part of the shock of the oil spill was that such a thing could happen in a country having such a sophisticated technology. The much overworked phrase "If we can send a man to the moon . . ." took on special meaning in Santa Barbara. When, in years previous, Santa Barbara's elected officials had attempted to halt the original sale of leases, "assurances" were given by Interior that such an "accident" could not occur, given the highly developed state of the industry. Not only did it occur, but the original gusher of oil spewed forth completely out of control for ten days, and the continual "seepage" which followed it remains uncontrolled to the present moment—seven months later. That the government would embark upon so massive a drilling program with such unsophisticated technology was shocking indeed.

Further, not only was the technology inadequate and the plans for stopping a leak, should one occur, nonexistent, but the area in which the drilling took place was known from the outset to be extremely hazardous. That is, drilling was occurring on an ocean bottom known for its extraordinary geological circumstances— porous sand lacking a bedrock "ceiling" capable of restraining uncontrollably seeping oil. Thus, the continuing leakage through the sands at various points above the oil reservoir cannot be stopped, and this could have been predicted from the data known to all parties involved.

Another peculiarity of the Channel that had been known to the experts is the fact that it is located in the heart of earthquake activity in a region which is among the most earthquake prone in the country. Santa Barbarans are now asking what might occur during an earthquake; if pipes on the ocean floor and casings through the ocean bottom should be sheared, the damage done by the Channel's thousands of potential producing wells would devastate the entire coast of Southern California. The striking contrast between the sophistication of the means used to locate and extract oil and the primitiveness of the means to control and clean its spillage became extremely clear in Santa Barbara.

Recurrent attempts have been made to ameliorate the continuing seep by placing floating booms around an area of leakage and then sending workboats to skim off the leakage from within the demarcated area. Chemical dispersants of various kinds have also been tried. But the oil bounces over the booms in the choppy waters, the workboats suck up only a drop in the bucket, and the dispersants are effective only when used in quantities which constitute a graver pollution threat than the oil they are designed to eliminate. Cement is poured into suspected fissures in an attempt to seal them up. Oil on the beaches is periodically cleaned by dumping straw over the sands and then raking it up along with the oil which it has absorbed. The common sight of men throwing straw on miles of beaches, within view of complex drilling rigs capable of exploiting resources thousands of feet below the ocean's surface, became a clear symbol to Santa Barbarans. They gradually began to see the oil disaster as the product of a system that promotes research and development in areas which lead to strategic profitability—without regard for social utility.

This kind of subordination of science to profit came out more directly in the workings of the Presidential committee of "distinguished" scientists and engineers (the DuBridge Panel) which was to recommend means of eliminating the seepage under Platform A. When the panel was appointed, hopes were raised that at last the scientific establishment of the nation would come forth with a technologically sophisticated solution to the problem. Instead, the panel —after a two-day session and after hearing no testimony from anyone not connected with either Oil or the Interior Department— recommended the "solution" of drilling an additional 50 wells under Platform A in order to pump the area dry as quickly as possible. One member of the panel estimated that the process would take from 10 to 20 years. Despite an immediate local clamor, Interior refused to make public the data or the reasoning behind the recommendations. The information on Channel geological conditions had been provided by the oil companies (the Geological Survey routinely depends upon the oil industry for the data upon which it makes its "regulatory" decisions). The data, being private property, thus could not be released—or so the government claimed. For Union Oil itself has given a clearance to the public release of the data. In this way both parties are neatly protected, while Santa Barbara's local experts remain thwarted by the counter-arguments of Oil/Interior that "if you had the information we have, you would agree with us."

Science played a similarly partisan role in other areas of the fight that Santa Barbarans were waging against the oil companies. The Chief Deputy Attorney General of California, for example, complained that the oil industry "is preventing oil drilling experts from aiding the Attorney General's office in its lawsuits over the Santa Barbara oil spill." Noting that his office had been unable to get assistance from petroleum experts at California universities, The Deputy Attorney General stated: "The university experts all seem to be working on grants from the oil industry. There is an atmosphere of fear. The experts are afraid that if they assist us in our case on behalf of the people of California, they will lose their oil industry grants."

At the Santa Barbara campus of the University, there is little oil money in evidence and few, if any, faculty members have entered into proprietory research arrangements with Oil. Petroleum geology and engineering is simply not a local specialty. Yet it is a fact that oil interests did contact several Santa Barbara faculty members with offers of funds for studies on the ecological effects of the oil spill, with publication rights stipulated by Oil. It is also the case that the Federal Water Pollution Control Administration explicitly requested a U.C. Santa Barbara botanist to withhold the findings of his study, funded by that agency, on the ecological effects of the spill.

Most of these revelations received no publicity outside of Santa Barbara. The Attorney's allegation, however, did become something of a state-wide issue when a professor at the Berkeley campus, in his attempt to refute the charge, actually confirmed it. Wilbur H. Somerton, professor of petroleum engineering, indicated he could not testify against Oil "because my work depends on good relations with the petroleum industry. My interest is serving the petroleum industry. I view my obligation to the community as supplying it with well-trained petroleum engineers. We train the industry's engineers and they help us."

Santa Barbara's leaders were incredulous about the whole affair. The question—one which is asked more often by the down-trodden sectors of the society than by the privileged—was posed: "Whose university is this, anyway?" A local executive and GOO leader asked, "If the truth isn't in the universities, where is it?" A conservative member of the state legislature, in a move reminiscent of SDS demands, went so far as to demand an end to all faculty "moonlighting" for industry. In Santa Barbara, the only place where all of this publicity was appearing, there was thus an opportunity for insight into the linkages between knowledge, the university, government and oil—and into the resultant non-neutrality of

science. The backgrounds of many members of the DuBridge Panel
were linked publicly to the oil industry. DuBridge himself, as a past
president of Cal Tech, served under a board of trustees which
included the president of Union Oil and which accepted substantial
Union Oil donations.

While "academic truth" was being called into question, some
truths not usually dwelt on by Oil's experts were gaining public
attention. In another of its front-page editorials, the News-Press set
forth a number of revealing facts about the oil industry. The combination of output restrictions, extraordinary tax write-off privileges
for drilling expenses, the import quota, and the 27 1/2 per cent depletion allowance creates an artificially high price for U.S. oil—a
price almost double the world market price for a comparable product delivered to comparable U. S. destinations. The combination of
available incentives creates a situation where some oil companies
pay no taxes whatsoever during extraordinarily profitable years. In
the years 1962-1966, Standard Oil of New Jersey paid less than four
per cent of its profits in taxes. Standard of California less than three
per cent, and 22 of the other largest oil companies paid slightly
more than six per cent. It was pointed out again and again to Santa
Barbarans that it was this system of subsidy which made the relatively high cost deep-sea exploration and drilling in the Channel
profitable in the first place. Thus the citizens of Santa Barbara, as
federal taxpayers and fleeced consumers, were subsidizing their own
eco-catastrophe.

[THE MECHANISMS OF DECEPTION]

The way in which federal officials and the oil industry frus-
trated the democratic process and thwarted popular dissent in
Santa Barbara is hardly unfamiliar. But the upper-middle-class
nature of the community, and the sharp features of an event which
was a sudden disruption of normality, make it an ideal case for
illustrating some of the techniques by which the powers that be
maintain the status quo.

The first of these has been described by Daniel Boorstin as the
technique of the "pseudo-event." A pseudo-event occurs when men
arrange conditions to simulate a particular kind of event so that
certain prearranged consequences follow as though the actual event

had taken place. Several pseudo-events took place in Santa Barbara. From the outset, it was obvious that national actions concerning oil were aimed at freezing out any local participation in decisions affecting the Channel. Thus, when the federal government first called for bids on a Channel lease in 1968, local officials were not even informed. Further, local officials were not notified by any government agency in the case of the original oil spill, nor (except after the spill was already widely known) in the case of any of the previous or subsequent more "minor" spills. The thrust of the federal government's colonialist attitude toward the local community was contained in an Interior Department engineer's memo released by Senator Cranston's office. Written to the Assistant Secretary of the Interior to explain the policy of refusing to hold public hearings prior to drilling, it said: "We preferred not to stir up the natives any more than possible."

The Santa Barbara County Board of Supervisors turned down the call for "participation" in drawing up new "tougher" drilling regulations precisely because they knew the government had no intention of creating "safe" drilling regulations. They refused to utilize "normal channels," refusing thereby to take part in the pseudo-event and thus to let the consequences (in this case the appearance of democratic decision-making and local assent) of a non-event occur.

There were other attempts to stage pseudo-events. Nixon's "inspection" of the Santa Barbara beachfront was an obvious one. Another series of such events were the congressional hearings set up by legislators who were, in the words of a well-to-do lady leader of GOO, "kept men." The locals were allowed to blow off steam at the hearings, but their arguments, however cogent, failed to bring about legislation appropriate to the pollution crisis. Many Santa Barbarans had a similar impression of the court hearings regarding the various legal maneuvers against oil drilling.

Another technique for diffusing and minimizing popular protest evidenced in the Santa Barbara affair might be called the "creeping event." A creeping event is, in a sense, the opposite of a pseudo-event. It occurs when something *is* actually taking place, but when the manifestations of the event are arranged to occur at an inconspicuously gradual and piecemeal pace, thus avoiding some of the consequences which would follow from the event if it were immediately perceived to be occurring.

The major creeping event in Santa Barbara was the piecemeal resumption of production and drilling after Hickel's second moratorium. Authorization to resume *production* at different specific groups of wells occurred on various dates throughout February and early March. Authorization to resume *drilling* of various groups of new wells was announced by Interior on dates from April 1 through August. Each resumption was announced as a particular safety precaution to relieve pressures, until finally on the most recent resumption date, the word "deplete" was used for the first time in explaining the granting of permission to drill. There is thus no *specific* point in time at which production and drilling were re-authorized for the Channel—and full resumption still has not been officially authorized.

A creeping event has the consequence of diffusing resistance by withholding what journalists call a "time peg" on which to hang the story. By the time it becomes quite clear that "something *is* going on," the sponsors of the creeping event (and the aggrieved themselves) can ask why there should be any protest "now" when there was none before, in the face of the very same kind of provocation. In this way, the aggrieved has resort only to frustration and the gnawing feeling that events are sweeping by him.

A third way of minimizing legitimate protest is by use of the alleged "neutrality" of science and the knowledge producers. I have discussed the "experts" and the University. After learning of the collusion between government and Oil and the use of secret science as a prop to that collusion, Santa Barbarans found themselves in the unenviable position of having to demonstrate that science and knowledge were not, in fact, neutral arbiters. They had to prove, *by themselves,* that continued drilling was not safe; that the "experts" who said it was safe were the hirelings, directly or indirectly, of oil interests; and that the report of the DuBridge Panel recommending massive drilling was a fraudulent document. They had to show that the university petroleum geologists themselves were in league with the oil companies and that information unfavorable to the oil interests was systematically withheld by virtue of the very structure of the knowledge industry. This is no small task. It is a long and complicated story, and one which pits lay persons (and a few academic renegades) against an entire profession and the patrons of that profession. An illustration of the difficulties involved may be drawn from very recent history. Seventeen Santa Barbara plaintiffs, represented by the ACLU, sought a temporary injunction against additional Channel drilling at least until the information utilized by the DuBridge Panel was made public and a hearing could be held. The injunction was not granted, and in the end the presiding federal judge ruled in favor of what he termed the "expert opinions available to the Secretary of the Interior. Due to limited time for rebuttal, the disorienting confusions of courtroom procedures, and also perhaps the desire not to offend the Court, the ACLU lawyer could not make his subtle, complex and highly controversial case that the "experts" were partisans and that their scientific "findings" followed from that partisanship.

A fourth obstacle was placed in the way of dissenters by the communications media. Just as the courtroom setting was not amenable to a full reproduction of the facts supporting the ACLU case, so the media in general—due to restrictions of time and style —prevented a full airing of the details of the case. A more cynical analysis of the media's inability to make known the Santa Barbara "problem" in its full fidelity might hinge on an allegation that the media were constrained by fear of "pressures" from Oil and its allies. Metromedia, for example, sent to Santa Barbara a team which spent several days documenting, interviewing and filming for an hour-long program—only to suddenly drop the project entirely due to what is reported by locals in touch with the network to have been "pressures" from Oil. Even without such blatant interventions, however, the full reproduction of the Santa Barbara "news" would remain problematic.

News media are notorious for the anecdotal nature of their reporting; even so-called "think pieces" rarely go beyond a stringing together of proximate events. There are no analyses of the "mobilization of bias" or linkages of men's actions with their pecuniary interests. Science and learning are assumed to be neutral; regulatory agencies are assumed to function as "watchdogs" for the public. Information contradicting these assumptions is treated as an exotic exception.

The complexity of the situations to be reported and the wealth of details needed to support such analyses require more time and effort than journalists have at their command. Their recitation would produce long stories not consistent with space limitations and make-up preferences of newspapers, or with analogous requirements within the other media. A full telling of the story would tax the reader/viewer and would risk boring him. The rather extensive media coverage of the oil spill centered on a few dramatic moments in its history (e.g., the initial gusher of oil) and a few simple-to-tell "human interest" stories such as the pathetic deaths of the sea birds struggling along the oil-covered sands. With increasing temporal and geographical distance from the initial spill, national coverage became increasingly rare and sloppy. Interior Department statements on the state of the "crisis" were reported without local rejoinders as the newsmen who might have gathered them began leaving the scene. While the Santa Barbara spill received extraordinarily extensive national coverage relative to other controversial events, this coverage nevertheless failed to adequately inform the American public about a situation which Santa Barbarans knew from first-hand experience.

Finally, perhaps the most pernicious technique of all because of the damage it does to the social conscience, is the routinization of evil. Pollution of the Santa Barbara Channel is now routine; the issue is not whether or not the Channel is polluted, but *how much* it is polluted. A recent oil slick discovered off a Phillips Oil platform in the Channel was dismissed by an oil company official as a "routine" drilling by-product which was not viewed as "obnoxious." That about half of the oil currently seeping into the Channel is allegedly being recovered is taken as an improvement sufficient to preclude the "outrage" that a big national story would require.

Similarly, the pollution of the moral environment becomes routine; it is accepted as natural that politicians are "on the take," "in the pockets of Oil." The depletion allowance remains a question of percentages (20 per cent of 27 1/2 per cent), rather than a focus for questioning the very legitimacy of such special benefits. "Compromises" emerge, such as the 24 per cent depletion allowance and the new "tough" drilling regulations, which are already being hailed as "victories" for the reformers. Like the oil spill itself, the depletion allowance debate becomes buried in its own disorienting detail, in its pseudo-events and in the triviality of the "solutions" which ultimately come to be considered as the "real" options. Evil is both banal and complicated, and each of these attributes contributes to its durability.

[THE MECHANISMS OF CHANGE]

What the citizens of Santa Barbara learned through their experience was that the parties competing to shape decision-making on oil in Santa Barbara do not have equal access to the means of "mobilizing bias." The Oil/Government combine had, from the start, an extraordinary number of advantages. Lacking ready access to media, the ability to stage events at will, and a well-integrated system of arrangements for achieving their goals (at least in comparison to their adversaries), Santa Barbara's citizens have met with repeated frustrations.

Their response to their relative powerlessness has been analogous to that of other groups and individuals who, from a similar vantage point, come to see the system up close. They become willing to expand their repertoire of means of influence as their cynicism and bitterness increase. Letter writing gives way to demonstrations, demonstrations to civil disobedience. People refuse to participate in "democratic procedures" which are a part of the opposition's event-management strategy. Confrontation politics arises as a means of countering official events with "events" of one's own, thus providing the media with stories which can be simply and energetically told.

Thus, in Santa Barbara, rallies were held at local beaches; congressmen and state and national officials were greeted by demonstrations. (Fred Hartley of Union Oil inadvertently landed his plane in the middle of one such demonstration, causing a rather ugly name-calling scene to ensue.) A "sail-in" was held one Sunday with a flotilla of local pleasure boats forming a circle around Platform A, each craft bearing large anti-Oil banners. City hall meetings were packed with citizens reciting demands for immediate and forceful local action.

A City Council election held during the crisis resulted in a landslide for the Council's bitterest critic and the defeat of a veteran councilman suspected of having "oil interests." In a rare action, the News-Press condemned the local Chamber of Commerce for accepting oil money for a fraudulent tourist advertising campaign which touted Santa Barbara (including its beaches) as completely restored to its former beauty.

One possible grand strategy for Santa Barbara was outlined by a local public relations man and GOO worker, who said, "We've got to run the oil men out. The city owns the wharf and the harbor that the company has to use. The city has got to deny its facilities to oil traffic, service boats, cranes and the like. If the city contravenes some federal navigation laws [which such actions would unquestionably involve], to hell with it. The only hope to save Santa Barbara is to awaken the nation to the ravishment. That will take public officials who are willing to block oil traffic with their bodies and with police hoses, if necessary. Then federal marshals or federal troops would have to come in. This would pull in the national news media."

This scenario has thus far not occurred in Santa Barbara, although the continued use of the wharf by the oil industries has led to certain militant actions. A picket was maintained at the wharf for two weeks to protest the conversion of the pier from a recreation and tourist facility into an industrial plant for the use of the oil companies. A boycott of other wharf businesses (e.g., two restaurants) was urged. The picket line was led by white, middle-class adults—one of whom was a local businessman who, two years earlier, was a close runner-up in the Santa Barbara mayoralty race.

Prior to the picketing, a dramatic Easter Sunday confrontation (involving approximately 500 persons) took place between demonstrators and city police. Just as a wharf rally was breaking up, an oil service truck began driving up the pier to make a delivery of casing supplies for oil drilling. There was a spontaneous sit-down in front of the truck. For the first time since the Ku Klux Klan folded in the '30s, a group of (heavily) middle-class Santa Barbarans was publicly taking the law into its own hands. After much lengthy discussion between police, the truck driver and the demonstrators, the truck was ordered away and the demonstrators remained to rejoice over their victory. The following day's News-Press editorial, while not supportive of such tactics, was quite sympathetic, which was noteworthy given the paper's long-standing bitter opposition to similar tactics when exercised by dissident Northern blacks or student radicals.

A companion demonstration on the water failed to materialize. A group of Santa Barbarans was to sail to the Union platform and "take it," but choppy seas precluded a landing, and the would-be conquerors returned to port in failure.

It would be difficult to predict what forms Santa Barbara's resistance will take in the future. A veteran News-Press reporter who covered the important oil stories has publicly stated that if the government fails to eliminate both the pollution and its causes, "there will, at best, be civil disobedience in Santa Barbara and at worst, violence." In fact, talk of "blowing up" the ugly platforms has been recurrent—and it is heard in all social circles.

But just as this kind of talk is not entirely serious, it is difficult to know the degree to which the other militant statements are meaningful. Despite frequent observations about the "radicalization" of Santa Barbara, it is difficult to determine the extent to which the authentic grievances against Oil have been generalized into a radical analysis of American society. Certainly an SDS membership campaign among Santa Barbara adults would be a dismal failure. But that is too severe a test. People, particularly basically contented people, change their world-view very slowly, if at all. Most Santa Barbarans still go about their comfortable lives in the ways they always have; they may even help Ronald Reagan win another term in the state house. But I do conclude that large numbers of persons have been moved, and that they have been moved in the direction of the radical left. They have gained insights into the structure of power in America not possessed by similarly situated persons in other parts of the country. It can be a revealing shock to experience an event first-hand and then to hear it described, and distorted, by the press and the government. People extrapolate from such experiences to the possibility that official descriptions of other events may be similarly biased and misleading. And when these questions arise, deeper ones follow. As a consequence some Santa Barbarans, especially those with the most interest in and information about the oil spill, while still surrounded by comfort and certainty, have nevertheless come to view power in America more intellectually, more analytically, more sociologically—more radically—than they did before.

_____

Harvey Molotch is an assistant professor of sociology at the University of California, Santa Barbara, specializing in urban ecology.

_____

[Ecology of Oil] Raping Alaska

Barry Weisberg

Americans would like to believe that the sins of Manifest Destiny are buried in the past, that the slaughter of the Indians and the extinction of the buffalo are but regretful memories, the stuff of history. But today in Alaska, this history is alive. There, drawn by the vast reservoir of oil discovered on the North Slope of the arctic coast, the awesome forces of American industry have assembled to re-enact the ruinous plunder of the great frontier.

To look at Alaska today is to return to a time when our waters ran pure, our landscape was unmarred by the oil derrick and the corner gas station, and the buffalo still roamed the open plains—Texas of 50 years ago or California before the turn of the century. What we are seeing in Alaska is a vivid compression of the past beauty and present devastation of the entire American environment.

To the popular mind Alaska—with 586,400 square miles, an area as large as California, Texas and Montana together—seems a vast, forbidding wasteland. In fact it is a land of incomparable beauty and resource, boasting endless cascades of timber, immortal rivers, mammoth glaciers; unbounded plains of caribou, grizzly bear, polar bear, and wolf; animals and plants unknown to most men. The amenities of clean air, water and pristine habitation are unrivaled anywhere else in the world.

Alaska's antiquity can be discovered in the immense solitude of her mountains. Three great ranges transverse this land, many glaciated and silent beneath the ages-old mantle of snow and ice. Contrary to the usual image, during several months of the year Alaska is laden with brilliant poppies, roses, wild flowers, and vast continuous multi-colored fields. Hardly a bleak and uninviting world!

Alaska has more coastline (34,000 miles) than all the other coastal states combined. There is potential here for an estuary agriculture that could feed millions. There is more timber, water, and

Illustrations by Gene Holtan

copper in Alaska than in all the rest of the United States combined. And, it appears, more oil.

On September 10, 1969, the corporate oil hustlers of the world descended on Anchorage for an unprecedented geological lottery in which they shelled out nearly a billion dollars—as much as $28,000 an acre—for a chance to exploit an oil field that may well turn out to be comparable to the massive field in the Middle East.

This peak price of $28,000 an acre was a respectable increase over the two cents an acre for which the U.S. purchased Alaska from Russia in 1867. As every school child knows, the area was originally meant to be kept as an icebox or a folly. But the discovery of gold at the turn of the century gave Alaska territorial status; in 1958, after many years of struggle by its white citizens, Alaska was granted statehood. Gold, fisheries and Government have brought with them the unwanted burdens of absentee landlordism. But it was not until early 1968, when oil was discovered around Prudhoe Bay on the northern arctic coast, that Alaska learned what real outside intervention was all about.

In 1965, '66, and '67, four major companies—Atlantic Richfield Company (Arco), British Petroleum (BP), Humble, a Jersey Standard subsidiary, and Sinclair—leased acreage for oil exploration on the North Slope, paying a total of 12 million dollars for leases now worth upwards of two *billion* dollars—or more than 150 times as much.

On February 16, 1968, Atlantic Richfield announced that its Prudhoe Bay No. 1 drilling rig, located two miles from the shores of the Arctic Ocean, had struck both oil and gas. Four months later, Arco's Sag River No. 1 rig, several miles to the southeast, struck oil.

In less than six months, a wilderness area the size of Massachusetts had been opened up to rapid development. In that time millions of pounds of equipment, fuel oil, pre-fabricated buildings, dynamite, people and food were flown in. Hundreds of miles of seismic lines had been run across the tundra, leaving permanent scars. And in a dramatic preview of the ecological disasters to come, a winter road was cut across the Alaskan wilderness to link Fairbanks with the Slope. The road, which was open for one month before it turned into the longest man-made swamp in the world, was officially named the Walter J. Hickel Highway.

Any objections to this "boom" raised by conservationists and others whom oil men find unaccountably superstitious about Industrial Progress, received a ready answer:

> "There is oil out there.
> Somebody has got to get it out.
> You may not believe this,
> but it will be good for your town,
> good for the people."

These particular lines were spoken by James Stewart in a movie (made long before the Santa Barbara oil catastrophe) about the world's first offshore drilling rig. But the same story has been given throughout history to every town and nation into whose land the oil industry has dug its iron claws: black gold will bring progress and prosperity.

Yet the Alaskan experience raises fundamental questions about this whole "development" process and the profit-oriented exploitation of resources—questions about the proper rate, purposes and forms of development, about who controls and benefits from it and by what right, and who really pays the price—questions about the heavy costs to life that do not show up on oil company balance sheets. These are the reservations that are obscured by the clichés of Progress, and overwhelmed by the euphoria of an economic "boom."

The $900 million paid to the State of Alaska at the September 10th oil lease auction was touted as a munificent offering on the part of the oil companies. In fact it was only a fraction of the land's actual value. If prior lease sales are any indication, present value of this acreage is closer to $5 billion. Long-range value may soar as high as $50 billion within a decade. And while the state is now slated to receive a small share of ongoing revenues—a 12.5 per cent royalty and a 4 per cent severance tax—calculations by Gregg Erickson, a University of Alaska resource economist, indicate that the "State's severance tax/royalty can be raised to the vicinity of 85 to 90 per cent and still leave the oil companies a better than 10 per cent

rate of return." The oil industries justify their profit by referring to the great risks they are taking in Alaska. But their claims are not terribly convincing. The journal Oil Week, in a much quoted statement, estimated that only five to ten billion barrels of oil were located in the Prudhoe Bay area. Yet over 50 per cent of the Alaskan' geology is acknowledged to lend itself to anti-clines, or oil-bearing structures. Interior Secretary Hickel, a well known partisan of oil, himself put the Alaskan reserves at about 100 billion barrels. Without question the Alaskan find will compare to, and likely dwarf, our primary domestic source today, the 30 billion-barrel East Texas find of the 1930's. Until Alaska, only 118 billion barrels of oil had been found in all of North America in the last 110 years.

This tremendous oil strike opens up the most perilous prospects for the Alaskan eco-system. No other industry could pose such a comprehensive threat to the wilderness environment of Alaska. No other industry can amass such large amounts of capital, or is so highly favored by tax laws. No other industry affects its environs as completely as does oil—its exploration, extraction, and transportation.

The significance of Alaskan oil development extends far beyond Alaska itself, carrying grave implications for our ecological well-being in its broadest sense, from the ongoing eco-catastrophe of our decaying, choked, polluted cities to the severe distortion in the allocation of basic ` global resources that American power imposes on the world. But to fully grasp these wider implications, one must first consider what the oil development means for ecology in the narrower sense, in the wilderness environment where the oil was found.

If oil is a uniquely devastating ecological enemy, Alaska is also a uniquely vulnerable victim. Until a very few years ago, Alaska remained essentially untouched by technological civilization. All of the organisms within its vast eco-system worked in complex and delicate symbiotic relations, species having survived and adjusted in accord with their ability to achieve symbiosis. Modern industrial society, on the other hand, works toward individuation and competition, toward conflict and instability. In the extreme but relatively stable and regular conditions of the arctic, the web of life-supporting relationships depends on the slimmest margins of sustenance.

The slender food chains and parsimonious life-cycles afford little tolerance for disruptions in the pattern of balance. The slightest manipulation of the life support system, the alteration of a bird migration, the pollution of a river, the noise of an airplane, all have incalculable unanticipated consequences. That is what makes this unique and irreplaceable eco-system so utterly fragile and so vulnerable to the careless intrusions of industrial man.

In natural systems, the discarded and unused substance of one organism becomes the energy of another. With our consumption cult and profit-oriented technology, we seek to abrogate that rule, manufacturing and depositing waste with abandon. Industrial man's mania for waste is particularly disastrous on the Alaskan tundra, where debris survives intact longer than it does any other place in the world. Orange peels last for months, paper for years, wood scraps for decades; metal or plastic is practically immortal. The reason for this longevity is that arctic eco-systems are not prone to "biograde," i.e., to decompose matter. Because of the extremely slow decomposition rate, and the slow healing capacity of the mat of vegetative cover called tundra, the littering and desecration that normally take years in other parts of the world can happen almost overnight in the arctic.

Damage to the tundra is irreversible. This blanket of surface vegetation is a protective covering that insulates the deep layer of permafrost below. The permafrost, a mass of gravel, ice and mud that begins about a foot beneath the surface and extends downward a thousand feet or more, remains frozen throughout the year, providing a solid ground beneath the tundra. But when the cover is stripped away, the permafrost melts, leaving an open, unhealing wound of mud, slush and water that tends to drain away, undermining the stability of large areas of the surrounding earth.

The record of Alaskan "development" is written clearly in the tundra. Scars gouged by bulldozers 15 years ago remain distinct today. At Point Barrow and Amchitka and at the abandoned Naval Petroleum Reserve number four, one can see miles upon miles of oil barrels, wrecked airplanes and autos, Quonset huts and undistinguished junk—most if not all government donated. This is not merely an aesthetic problem. "Even now, 25 years later," says one observer, "many men who long ago left the Arctic still kill wildlife by the partially empty fuel drums they left behind. If conditions are right, they may wipe out an acre or two, or with luck, a whole lake."

But if the oil barrel in Alaska seems to some an ominous talisman foretelling environmental disaster, it is welcomed by others almost as an adornment. Colonel E. L. Hardin, chief of the Army corps of engineers in Alaska, says cheerfully, "The fifty-five gallon oil drum is the new state flower of Alaska." And the depth of the oil industry's concern for the environment, as well as the extent of its designs on it, is captured nicely in the response of one executive upset by the damage done by company equipment: "If we go on like that we won't have the remotest chance of getting into the wildlife range." However, rumors of clandestine explorations in the arctic national wildlife refuge abound.

Driving the Hickel Highway

There is little in the record of the oil development so far to inspire confidence in the future. The Hickel Highway fiasco—Hickel's last official act as governor—was only a hint of disasters to come. The road was to provide access to the Slope in winter when shipping is blocked and supplies must be flown in. It was a risky project at best, but the route was laid in what were obviously the worst areas, those with soils having the highest ice concentrations. When the ice broke up as summer approached, the permafrost melted and water from the adjacent land poured onto the roadbed, where it remains today. Hickel's response to critics was: "So they've scarred the tundra. That's one road, 12 feet wide, in an area as big as the state of California."

Years ago the extraction of any resource meant the establishment of a technological enclave, isolated for the most part from its surroundings. That at least was the model. Today oil extraction brings with it a whole supporting complex of advanced technology —"advanced" indicating that it is less restricted by or adapted to the natural environment and more able to impose its imperatives on the landscape, leaving it to nature to attempt to restore the ecological balance.

The primary challenge to the industry in this respect is transporting the oil to market once it is brought up from the ground. Roughly half of what the industry will spend exploiting Alaskan oil will go to providing transportation for it.

Plans are well underway for the construction of the Trans Alaska Pipeline Systems (TAPS). This $900 million pipeline will run from the North Slope some 800 miles across the Alaskan interior down to Valdez, an ice-free port on the Pacific southern coast. Described by the contractors as the "largest single construction feat in the free world," the pipeline will eventually transport some two million barrels of oil per day, at a temperature of 150°-170°. If placed underground, the builders admit that the line would melt all permafrost within a 25-foot radius. The actual pipeline trunk involves some 20,000 acres of land, but the roots necessary to support the venture will require another 7 to 9 million acres, accommodating 5 to 12 pumping stations, several landing fields, camp and administrative sites, microwave stations and access roads to the pipeline.

As noted in testimony given before the Department of Interior hearing in Fairbanks last August, "The construction and operation of a large, buried, hot [the oil must be heated to flow freely] pipeline in permafrost regions has never been done anywhere in the world." Of the many elements of arctic development, none has as great a potential for gross disturbance of the entire eco-system as does this pipeline. Laid upon a ten-foot bed of gravel (gravel taken from river beds, thus upsetting spawning and other cycles), it will almost certainly generate vast problems for soil stability in the permafrost— both because any intervention is hazardous to the delicate balance and because the varying ice contents of the soil require differing specifications for construction. The dangers of erosion, subsidence and stress to the surrounding environs are critical. Animals rely upon the vegetative cover for food and oxygen. To upset that balance is to intervene in the life-supporting processes of the entire biological chain of the arctic.

Wildlife patterns can be disturbed in an infinite number of ways. The mere physical obstruction of the pipeline itself would constitute a perilous barrier to the region's 400,000 caribou, blocking the migrations that are an integral and inescapable part of their life. To interfere with this ageless process invites a repetition of the fate of the buffalo.

This is only the beginning. Alongside the pipeline, the so-called "corridor concept" of development which TAPS is encouraging will string roads, railways, material storage centers and small settlements—and thus the inevitable forms of sprawl which follow such corridors. To talk about the pipeline, then, is to talk about an 800-mile strip of development, gross disturbance of eco-systems, and the basic interference with many life-giving cycles of the arctic.

From the same people
who brought you Santa Barbara

On top of TAPS, the eagerness to get the crude petroleum out of Alaska to market has spawned the legendary voyage of the *Manhattan,* the 115,000-deadweight-ton super tanker that successfully passed through the arctic ice pack from the east coast of the United States to Point Barrow, Alaska, just west of the Prudhoe Bay oil area. Although the oil companies cited it as one of the "risks" of Alaskan development, they had already ordered eight more gigantic tankers before the first journey was completed. More than 1000 feet long, the *Manhattan* is able to crush its way through 40-foot-thick arctic ice. And orders are in for oil tankers three times as large. These technological behemoths—which in the course of their normal operations spew oil slick bilge and exhaust wastes in their wake—will cut a path of major disruption through more than a thousand miles of the arctic. As David Hickok, associate director of the Federal Field Commission for Development Planning in Alaska, notes, with such massive ocean-going ventures already in the works, there still exists an almost complete "lack of research and investigation in arctic waters on oil pollution, coastal processes, phytoplankton, marine fisheries and mammal populations, and on programs for the development of new technologies for port facilities in the arctic. All of these are prerequisite matters for governmental attention brought in focus by the voyage of the *Manhattan* and the granting of offshore exploratory drilling permits on the continental shelf. . . ."

Over and over the oil industry ends up repeating, "No one could reasonably have expected": the million ton spill on the Delaware beaches; the splitting open of the Ocean Eagle in the San Juan Harbor; the collision which poured 30,000 gallons into the waters off the Cape of Good Hope; or the spill from the Torrey Canyon "whose captain ran her onto a well-marked granite reef off England in broad daylight, causing the biggest shipwreck and oil pollution ever." Or Santa Barbara! Such "unanticipated hazards" mark the operations of the petroleum industry daily. And to add to the peril, the petro-chemical industry is considering transporting pesticides (a by-product of crude petroleum) in similar large tankers. We are told that if the Torrey Canyon had been carrying pesticides rather than oil, the effect of such a shock could have abruptly terminated the production of oxygen by photosynthesis in the entire North Sea.

The gap between our ability to devastate and our ability to heal is enormous. In Santa Barbara, the highly complex equipment dedicated to pumping oil out of the ground contrasts sharply with the technology used to clean it up (i.e., hay spread across the sands), and in cases like the Santa Barbara Channel or the Hickel Highway, the damage is permanent, beyond repair in the time of man. To guard against such disasters would require time and the development of new technology—costly tasks that bring no profit to the industries involved.

In Alaska (where costs are high even when corners are cut), ecological precautions are certainly not allowed to interfere with profits. This assessment emerged from Senate hearings on Alaska:

"Very frankly, in recent weeks, the committee [Senate Committee on Interior and Insular Affairs] has received a number of disturbing reports that present limitations on personnel and funding make it highly unlikely that proper environmental, conservation and safety control in connection with activities now underway or proposed will be fulfilled. I am hopeful that these reports are not true." It is a fleeting hope; anyone at all familiar with Alaska knows it is a futile one.

In Alaska today we are playing recklessly with forces which affect the entire planet. The arctic ice pack, for example, is perhaps the single most important land mass in determining global weather. It is possible that our interference with arctic heat patterns in the ice pack and the ocean (through oil explorations and transport) could upset basic weather balances affecting the height of the world's oceans, the amounts of rainfall, and other interdependent climatic functions.

There are all the symptoms of fatal pride in our tampering with these great harmonies. Thomas Kelly, the state official who presided over the big Alaska lease sale, was surely moved by hubris when he proclaimed, "To say that it is tundra today and should be tundra forever when tundra has no economic value doesn't make sense." Ted Stevens, appointed U.S. Senator in 1968 by then Governor Hickel, outdid Kelly in a speech before a meeting of the American Association for the Advancement of Science in Fairbanks last August. Stevens delivered a searing attack upon the ecologists who had come to discuss the oil development. After deriding out-of-state visitors as carpet-bag conservationists, he pulled out a dictionary and referred to the definition of ecology: "Ecology deals with the relationships between living organisms." "But," exclaimed the senator, "there are no living organisms on the North Slope."

Among the living organisms in Alaska which state officials would rather not think about are the native Eskimos, Aleuts and Indians, whose land the U.S. "bought" from Russia a century ago, and who still make up a sixth of Alaska's 272,000 population. According to the Statehood Act of 1958, 140 million acres of land were to be returned to the natives over a 25-year period. Years passed and the Alaskan native came to see clearly that the only way the white man could be made to live up to his 1958 "bargain" was through pressure. In 1966 the movement for native power coalesced into the Alaskan Federation of Natives, and their demands were formulated in the Alaska Native Land Claim bill.

In important respects, it was already too late. In 1964 the state, realizing that the North Slope was a potentially rich oil reserve, and that native pressure was mounting, applied to the Federal Bureau of Land Management (BLM) for the two million acres lying along the arctic coast in the Prudhoe Bay vicinity.

Although the land was a traditional hunting and fishing ground for the Eskimos, the state application claimed that it was free of aboriginal use and occupancy. The BLM then proceeded to publish notice of the state's intent in Jessens Weekly, a small mimeographed newspaper with irregular circulation. Thus, as Alaskan journalist Jane Bender comments, "The burden of proof was placed upon people who could not be expected to untangle the legal phraseology, who might not even have seen the notice in the first place, and whose knowledge of the far reaching consequences of that simple small print notice might be said to be minute."

The North Slope case was typical; the attitude of most white Alaskans is little better than colonial. So it is not surprising that the native claims have suffered continual erosion in the hands of all levels of government. In the first compromise the natives settled for 80 million acres; they were then forced down to 40 million acres. Walter Hickel now suggests 27 million and the governor, Keith Miller, suggests 13 million acres—out of the total of 365 million in the state—3.6 per cent of the land for a sixth of the population, when rightfully they own it all.

It is safe to assume that the empires of oil will wield their vast power to delay a native settlement. For if significant portions of the state were in the hands of the natives, the oil combine would have to deal with them rather than the state, and they are potentially much less willing accomplices in the rape of the land—as evidenced by their picketing at the lease sale.

Meanwhile there is increasing pressure to lift the freeze on land giveaways to state and private interests that was imposed by former Interior Secretary Udall pending a settlement of the native claims. For example, the TAPS pipeline by law must secure a lifting of the

freeze in order to proceed. However, as a New York Times editorial reports, "There is good reason to believe that preliminary work on the right of way has been started, without benefit of permit or of law."

Of course the oil industry has every reason to be confident that the government will smooth the way for it in Alaska. The $20 billion a year industry is famous for its unsurpassed political and economic power in America. Its lobbying muscle in Congress is legendary. It enjoys the lowest effective tax rate of any U.S. industry (seven per cent for the 23 largest companies). The oil depletion allowance is a prime symbol of corporate privilege, yet tax reform on it has been held to a meaningless reduction of a few percentage points. (Because of existing restrictions most large companies use only 24 per cent out of the current 27 1/2 per cent allowance anyway.)

An industry that has been able (notably through the Rockefeller-Standard Oil complex) to treat the U.S. State Department as a subsidiary headquarters, and at whose bidding America brings down sovereign governments (as in Iran), should not expect to have much trouble making its way in Alaska. Still, as extra insurance against public clamor, Atlantic-Richfield (which made the first North Slope strike) and other companies are investing large sums in advertising, and even in conservation groups, in an effort to control public awareness of key development issues.

The industry had little difficulty getting someone sympathetic to and familiar with their Alaska problems into the key Interior Department post. It is generally accepted in Washington that Atlantic-Richfield's chairman, Robert Anderson (who as Secretary of the Navy encouraged the opening of Alaskan lands to private development), was most responsible for President Nixon's appointment of Hickel to Interior. Certainly Hickel, with his celebrated oil connections, and his financial interests in the copper of the Brooks Mountain Range and the Yukon River Delta—another potential oil reserve—was not appointed for objectivity, nor for public relations finesse on conservation, given his plans to "build a Fifth Avenue on the tundra."

But the critical importance of the industry's political power in Alaskan development is most clearly revealed in an enormous irony: it is only the industry's ability to use government regulation to rig the American oil market that assures the profitability of exploiting Alaskan oil in the first place. It is, in other words, the artificial overcharges imposed on consumers, rather than its intrinsic economic profitability, that is underwriting the current rapid development of Alaskan oil and the environmental disruption that goes with it.

The rigging mechanism involved is the Oil Import Quota Program, which is conservatively estimated to cost the American consumer $4 billion a year. Production costs for oil from Texas and other domestic U.S. sources are far higher than those from rich, easily worked foreign reserves such as Venezuela or the Middle East. Even when the cost of transporting foreign oil to the U.S. is added on, its price at the point of delivery here is little more than 60 per cent that of domestically produced oil. The price of a barrel of comparable crude oil delivered to Philadelphia is about $2.25 for Mid-East compared to $3.75 for domestic. Allowing foreign oil to compete freely in the U.S. would drive all but the cheapest and most efficiently produced domestic oil out of the market. Instead, the government obligingly sets severe limits (presently 21 per cent of domestic consumption) on the amount of oil that can be imported. All oil in the U.S. is then sold to the consumer at the high prices of domestic oil.

Alaskan oil, according to current cost projections, is expected to be too expensive in production and transportation to compete on the world market with Middle Eastern and other oil. However Alaska is a state, and Alaskan oil is therefore domestic American oil. Thus, like the privileged petroleum of Texas, it can be sold in unlimited quantities at the artificially inflated prices of the U.S. market.

In a sense the current Alaskan Development can be considered an elaborate economic charade, in that profits come under the industry's power to levy exorbitant prices against the consumer, rather than from the normal proceedings of business. We would all be better off, in fact, just to pay the extra money directly into the corporate treasuries, plus a little bit to the State of Alaska in lieu of royalties, and have the companies leave the Alaskan environment alone.

It is quite possible, of course, that as time goes by and the impact of the magnitude of Alaska's reserves is felt, the cost of Alaskan oil will come down to an economically competitive level. The fact remains, however, that the financially riskless, headlong development we are seeing depends on the industry's ability to supersede the laws of the marketplace and to have its way in the affairs of men.

While there are stirrings of opposition to what is happening in Alaska, they are largely isolated and, consequently, impotent. Many legislators told me privately that they thought the oil lease sale should have been postponed but were afraid to say so publicly for fear of losing re-election. The Federal Field Commission for Development Planning in Alaska has repeatedly advocated more planning, more care, and a slower pace—to no avail. One legislator said, "The trouble is that the state government has said so little about the problems of the North Slope that I can't tell if they are ignorant, unconcerned or are withholding information for other reasons."

In Alaska, as elsewhere, the tremendous power of the oil industry over social development grows not only from its impressive ability to dictate government policy, but also from the extent to which patterns of development are set autonomously by the "private" operations of industry. It is the general void of public policy that gives industry a free hand to shape the future in terms of its private priorities, unchecked by public interest or authority. When government does intervene (usually under the influence of industry anyway), it is merely responding to the reality that industry has created.

There is virtually no public policy governing the pattern of social growth on the Alaskan frontier; there is no involvement by the people of Alaska or of the rest of the country, no informal advocacy procedure by which to evaluate what the oil companies are doing. As a result, oil exploration and production proceed in Alaska without any projected land use plan, without any legislative priorities for growth. There exist no uniform codes for oil and mineral exploration, no systematic efforts toward the preservation of wildlife populations, nor any air or water quality standards to speak of.

This abdication of public discretion is not an accident. David Hickok complains, "Both industry and government are deliberately preventing the operation of a public forum until after the important decisions are made." The problem, then, is not that our current situation results from no planning, for clearly the oil companies have a very keen sense of plan and purpose. It is rather that the plans which do exist are created and executed without public scrutiny or control.

In just "going about its business," the oil industry will change the face of Alaska more thoroughly than all the volumes of hotly debated social legislation that give people the illusion of controlling their own destiny. Meetings have been summoned throughout

Alaska by the Brookings Institution and the Stanford Research Institute to discuss the state's development plan. By invitation, participants will be discussing the future while oil is already determining it.

The coming of the oil empire to Alaska brings with it the vast support of operations of railroads, airlines, communications networks, new towns, urban growth and the like. Requiring highly skilled labor, these operations will not draw primarily on either natives or local whites. Consequently, entire communities of technically skilled men will be brought into Alaska: 5000 on the Slope, 3000 for the pipeline, 1500 at Valdez, hundreds more administrative persons in Anchorage and Fairbanks—all of them requiring housing, food, and related services. What will happen when initial construction of the new industry is completed and they leave? What will be the effect on the economy when some 10,000 people who have been disbursing enormous amounts of capital pull out in one year? The initial boom-town profits to local businessmen and landholders will give way to the ghost towns that followed the gold rush. The oil rush economy does not build for posterity.

Already the landscape of Alaska is dominated by a crude mix of the worst Texas gulf coast and Southern California plasticity. Housing is composed almost entirely of imported pre-fabricated units or trailers. A ticky-tacky frontier bar atmosphere permeates every Alaskan town. Within a very short time oil has penetrated all aspects of the Alaskan economy. In terms of outright ownership, the industry is gobbling up local business interests at a rapid rate. The income of hotels, restaurants and airlines depends upon the oil companies. The universities are in their employment.

The economic reality of oil development in Alaska is that control of the revenue (perhaps $100 billion in the next decade) implies power over social development. The unchecked nature of this power must force us to reconsider our whole system of ownership and extraction of resources. For instance—to consider the minimal alternative—if this oil were to be developed by a quasi-public corporation (looking to the TVA as one example), the revenue involved could be employed to initiate environmental quality regulatory programs or the reconstruction of urban cores. The present arrangement abdicates what may turn out to be the only source of revenue the United States could ever have to begin to cope with urban pathology. We presently act as if the oil were ordained by geology just to serve the industry, as if the oil companies somehow owned the oil which they sell to the people of the world at such fabulous profits.

The oil finds in the Arctic are tremendously important in themselves, but it is the dynamic they lock us into that sweeps out to affect the lives of every single person in the United States, and throughout most of the world. The results are simply taken for granted, without regard for the decisions that initiated them. The fact that oil development fixes the American landscape into transport corridors geared to accommodate cars, and only cars, is no small matter. For to insure the presence of the auto is to insure the persistence of current forms of urban sprawl. To pressure against cooperative modes of transit is to fix the shape of the city for tomorrow.

The technology of the automobile itself is obviously tightly meshed with that of oil. Cars presently consume upwards of two-fifths of all the crude oil produced. And it is clear that the environmental pollution that goes with the internal combustion engine and other petroleum-funded technology is not a mere matter of irritation or inconvenience. The head of the American Petroleum Institute's 300-member Committee on Air and Water Conservation continues to decry the "passion" and "emotionalism" which mark opposition to air pollution. He has said that "we can go along as we are now for another 10 to 15 years." But University of California Zoology Professor Kenneth E. F. Watt predicts, "It is now clear that air pollution concentrations are rising in California at a rate such that mass mortality incidents can be expected in specific areas, such as Long Beach, by the 1975-76 winter. The proportion of the population which will die in these incidents will at first equal, then exceed, that for the 1952 smog disaster." (Nearly 2500 Londoners died from the effects of smog during the Christmas season of that year.)

Already the children of Los Angeles are not allowed to "run, skip or jump" inside or outside on smog alert days, by order of the L.A. Board of Education and County Medical Association. If the oil and auto industries had spent a fraction of their advertising budgets on research for a smog-free engine, our air today might be safe for future generations.

Oil is at the core of the whole of American industry. Crude petroleum is the basis for the production of hydro-carbon feedstock and other basic petro-chemical industries. Petrol is the stuff from which roads, paints, detergents, synthetic rubber, cosmetics, nylon and pesticides are made. From its powerful position at the center, the oil industry fuels, sustains and protects the economy of waste on which its profits are based. It defends and expands that economy's myriad patterns of devastation: the private auto, in use about one per cent of the time and junked at a rate of 12 million a year, usurps 50 per cent of the space in our overcrowded cities with its highways and parking requirements; the use of DDT and other less celebrated pesticides generates crop surpluses which are then withheld from the hungry at home and abroad; the ubiquitous plastic packaging is neither reusable nor decomposable, and it pollutes the air when burned. This is the technology with which we are "developing" Alaska and civilizing the world. This technology costs $ 11 billion annually in damage to private property from air pollution alone.

The headlong rush of Alaskan development is part of a momentum that completely contradicts our knowledge about the capacity of the earth to support us—namely, that the resources of the earth are fixed; that, rather than continuous growth merely to accommodate the increasingly false consumptive needs of an increasing number of people, growth must be directed to achieve very specific public priorities—priorities which are determined by the kind of life-styles which neighborhoods and regions determine are best for them. Limits must be set. Development as it now proceeds minimizes the alternatives open to people, increasing the uniformity and standardization of life. It locks us into patterns over which we have little knowledge or control.

It is not enough merely to slow down in Alaska, as a New York Times editorial of November 10 argued. Development as it proceeds on the North Slope, and on countless other frontiers of American industry, must be curtailed. Until such time as the American public has adequate time and information to evaluate and assess the total costs of industrial development to all the people affected by it, development and the myth of growth must be curtailed. Rational resource consumption and re-cycling alone would eliminate the need for any further oil extraction on the face of the earth.

While the population of the world is expected to double in 35 years, it will consume resources at not twice, but five times the present rate, producing a scarcity in food and fossil fuels that will be the major source of friction in the coming decade. This results directly from consumptive patterns generated by the United States. It is the disequilibrium between man and nature, not the biologic process of procreation, which is at the root of the population issue. To cope with population is first and foremost an issue of coping with the current American imperialist consumption of 70 per cent of the world's resources by less than 7 per cent of the world's population.

The largest single consumer of crude petroleum is the American military—those who are charged with defending this squandering of other people's resources. Alaska is key to their continued world supremacy. As America shifts in Southeast Asia and throughout the world to air power rather than ground forces, the military appetite for oil will grow and will seek stable sources. Walter Levy, known as the dean of U.S. oil experts, points out, "A world power which depends on potentially reluctant or hostile countries for food and fuel that must travel over highly vulnerable sea routes is by definition no world power." While we "own" major portions of Mid-East reserves already, the transport of this oil is in constant jeopardy, as the closing of the Suez in 1967 showed. And domestic production, aside from Alaska, is projected to fall behind consumption at an increasing rate in the next few years. Alaskan reserves will stabilize the strategic military supply of crude oil. Moreover, as America prepares for the rearmament of Japan to help police Asia, treaty negotiations are already being pursued in Washington to provide Japan with a stable oil flow from Alaska in exchange for military and trade arrangements.

What Americans must realize is that the destruction of our life support systems will not be halted through our individual refusal to drive cars or use pesticides. As is evidenced by the Alaskan oil rush, development no longer proceeds along enclave lines, but is comprehensive in impact and scope, so that conservation efforts which act to preserve wilderness enclaves as parks or wildlife refuges will in the end lose those areas to the all-inclusive effects of air pollution, noise, and pesticides. The oil industry, virtually a world government, presides over an economy organized toward the destruction of life. Its power must be broken, not merely circumvented. The avenues of oil must be reached at their point of production, not merely in our own individual use.

If anything is to be learned from Alaska, it is that it is time to stop. Domination through growth has mesmerized the American mind for so long that the suggestion of curtailing growth is unthinkable. Greek rationalism, the Roman engineering mentality, the Biblical injunction to conquer and subdue nature, the post-Enlightenment mystique about technical progress—all espouse development.

Yet the old myth that continued growth increases our control over the environment is now simply false. We are losing control. We are destroying the air we breathe, the water we drink, and the land we walk upon. And this is not an accident. It is rooted in the fundamental attitudes and practices of advanced industrial society. It is in part the logic of capitalism, but it is more than that; it is the very relationship we assume toward the natural world.

The talk about shifting from an economy of affluence, obsolescence, redundancy and waste to an economy that recognizes scarcity must yield practical proposals for a new economics. And these proposals must include the mandatory re-cycling of all natural resources; the mandatory production of only re-cyclable containers; the rationing of all natural resources—rationing to provide for sane limits on the amount of consumption as well as to equalize mechanisms for distribution.

Industrial processes must be rationed as to the amount of oxygen, water or minerals they can consume in production. These are no small matters, but they are only the basic parameters for what would be the beginning of a truly democratic policy for our life support systems. The "economy of death" must be replaced by an economy of life.

Continued rapid development such as that in Alaska can only work for the forces of exploitation and greed. Time must be had to examine and consider every aspect of the development process, to create a comprehensive democratically determined land use policy, to devise environmental regulatory agencies with adequate means of enforcement, to develop new forms of revenue sharing and community control over economic growth, to re-learn our inclinations toward nature and our relationship to people unlike ourselves. While this must happen in Alaska, it must also happen on a national and global level. For clearly the powers that shape the fate of Alaska are rooted in places far distant from that beautiful land.

We must slow down. We must come to enjoy the world gently, remembering that this fragile earth is more to be admired than used, more to be cherished than exploited. Alaska teaches us that there are men for whom this is impossible. They must be stopped. Not for their sake, but for ours.

———————————

Barry Weisberg is a free-lance writer and co-director of the Bay Area Institute. David Kolodney is an editor of Ramparts.

———————————

California Water Plan:

The Most Expensive Faucet

in the World

Gene Marine

One of the most striking things about the ecology bandwagon is that it is becoming badly overpopulated with politicians who a year ago wouldn't have known a food chain from a string of supermarkets. Ecology is, these people assure us, a "safe" issue, best discussed in tones of restrained alarm and good also for distracting the gullible young from the war in Vietnam.

This just goes to show how little politicians understand the implications of what they've gotten themselves involved in. By its own inevitable logic, an ecological conscience must lead to revolutionary conclusions. And these conclusions will surely be hastened by the politicians' own acts. Selling off a whole area's precious water supply to satisfy certain highrollers who are big in the parapolitics of state power is a good example.

Water is neither as clean nor as free as it seems. And when combined with financial power, it becomes a highly volatile substance which does odd things—like flow through the hands of the people into the pockets of a few. In California, water is power. Water is wealth. These are just the most obvious lessons to be learned from the celebrated California Water Plan, which is also a carefully drawn blueprint for ecological disaster.

To understand this disaster, you first have to understand the nature of the ownership of California's major industry—agriculture. When you talk about California agriculture, you're not talking

Illustrations by Dave Sheridan

about farmers—at least not the individual, tilling his few hundred acres, normally conjured up by that term. There are those farmers in California—in numbers, a lot of them—and they do dominate a few specialty crops. But real agricultural wealth, which *is* the wealth of the state, lies in the hands of those "farmers" who own most of the land. In California, agriculture is synonymous with corporate empire: 79 per cent of the land is owned by seven per cent of the "farmers."

As agriculture—or agribusiness, if you want to insist on that accurate but repellent word—is the wealth of California, so is it the power. The power structures of New York, Illinois and Pennsylvania are complex. California's is simple—simpler, in fact, than Mississippi's and almost as simple as Honduras'. The people who own the land (not really people, of course: corporations) own the state.

California's aerospace industry, which seems to the casual observer to be extremely important in her economy and therefore in her politics, had prime contracts during the 1968-69 fiscal year (mostly from the Department of Defense and NASA) totaling around $7.5 billion. But by the time California's 200 commercial crops are harvested, transported, processed and packed, their market value is about $16 billion—and almost all that work is done inside the state.

Furthermore, if you search the list of contributors to any major candidate in the state and then run down the occupations of the people whose names you uncover, you'll find only small (and then probably personal) participation by aerospace people. You'll find the "farmers," though, every time—the "farmers" and the oilmen, who are often the same people and who in any case get along together very well. Add in the public utilities and the banks which are intricately tied in with the agricultural giants, and you have the power line-up. And it is these agricultural giants and their allies who, in an effort to control California's water (that precious commodity key to farm wealth) have brought the state to the brink of ecological disaster.

As a glance at any California map will show (a relief map makes it even easier), the Sacramento River, flowing from the north, and the San Joaquin River, flowing from the south, come together to form San Francisco Bay and ultimately to reach the ocean (actually, they don't any more, but that's later in the story). Where they come together is called, in California, "the Delta." The two valleys are thus not separated, and together are called simply the Central Valley.

The Sacramento Valley has, and has always had, enough water to handle agriculture on all its available land and more; but vast acres of the San Joaquin Valley were naturally damned to aridity. The availability of water diminishes sharply as you move south past the Delta. In the 1930's, however, the federal government undertook the gigantic Central Valley Project (CVP) to move "surplus" water from the north into the San Joaquin Valley—and precipitated a fight that lasted for decades and whose implications may be felt for centuries.

The CVP was built under the Reclamation Act of 1902, as subsequently amended. The 1862 Homestead Act provided settlers with a quarter section of land—160 acres—and the Reclamation Act provided for irrigation projects which would deliver to each supposedly small farmer enough water for 160 acres. But because of a number of unanticipated circumstances—vast swindles under the Swamp and Overflow Land Act; huge tracts given away by the federal government for railroads to encourage expansion; and a tangled mess of claims to old Mexican land grants—more than half of California's arable land passed into the hands of huge landowners before small farmers had a chance at it. During the Depression, even as CVP construction of dams and canals for the transfer of water was under way, bank foreclosures added other small holdings to the large tracts.

The Central Valley Project, however, will still deliver to any single landowner only enough water for 160 acres (320 acres if the landowner is married—a dubious but generous concession by the Bureau of Reclamation). If you own, say, 100,000 acres, you can

get water to irrigate the entire amount *only* if you agree to sell off all the acreage over 160 within ten years.

Now the mightier landowners, all-powerful within California's borders, tried for more than a decade to break the federal government's determination to stick to the 160-acre limitation regarding water rights. Unsuccessful, they did succeed at least in keeping CVP out of the west side of the San Joaquin Valley. These lands still sit aridly awaiting the water that to their owners is gold, and awaiting the day when that water will come without pesky federal regulation.

In 1959, when the California Water Plan was placed by legislative decision on the 1960 ballot, these were a few of the west side landowners:

Standard Oil Co. of Calif.	218,000 acres
Other oil companies, combined	264,000 acres
Kern County Land Co.	348,000 acres
Southern Pacific Railroad	200,000 acres
Tejon Ranch Company	348,000 acres
Boston Ranch Company	37,000 acres

And 1,323,000 other acres were in the hands of people who each owned more than 1000 acres. There is oil on some of this land, but it is not as valuable as the crops which, if water were available, could be grown there.

One institution which doesn't appear on the above list but which is indispensable to it is the Bank of America, by deposits the world's largest commercial bank (and itself a large landowner in agricultural California as a whole). The bank finances more than half of all California agriculture. Its former president, Rudolph Peterson, said late in 1968 that the Bank of America was "the world's largest agricultural lender with lines of credit for agricultural production running at about a billion dollars a year." The total commitment of the bank to agriculture is probably more than $3 billion. Rival banks, notably Wells Fargo, have large fingers in the pie, as do other "farmers" like Safeway Stores, Inc., the DiGiorgio Corporation and newcomers like Purex, Dow Chemical and United Fruit. Already for decades the absolute masters of California, these giants were still searching in the late '40's and early '50's, as they are today, for more and greater sources of agricultural wealth. Blocked by the Bureau of Reclamation's 160-acre limitation from any hope of federal subsidy for irrigation of their lands, they first tried unsuccessfully to get the state to finance the entire CVP itself without the federal government, and to give them the water without the 160-acre restriction. But Washington refused to cooperate, and the Big Guys had to look for other tills to tap.

The Central Valley Project's principal features were built by the early '50's and no one was in danger of dying of thirst or going out of business. A rational state power structure might have decided that a point of balance had been reached; that they were getting moderately rich in an effortless sort of way and it was time to sit back and consolidate gains. But rationality has never been the strong suit of power structures. And what was good for California was not good—or at least not good enough—for business. The major discontent came from the southern part of the state.

Southern California hustlers—especially the Los Angeles variety—are a special breed. They have, among other things, perfected the arts of luring people (wealthy people, preferably, although those with retirement savings are also nice) into their part of the state and selling them things (especially real estate). Somebody builds a new apartment house; he gives tenants a month's free rent for moving in; and as soon as it's built and full, he sells it to a little old lady from Iowa. Until this particular con was stopped recently, some couples boasted that they hadn't paid a month's rent in Los Angeles for three years. What you don't do is tell prospective immigrants that Los Angeles sits partly on a thinly covered desert basis, in the shadow of achingly eroded hills that could (and often do) slide down at any minute, bringing their precarious burden of houses with them. You advertise the new suburbs and don't talk about the fact that if there were any reason to live in those locations there probably wouldn't be *new* suburbs there at this late date. Above all, you don't tell them that Los Angeles outran its meager natural water supply more than a half century ago; that the water since stolen from Northern California's Owens Valley and conned from the Colorado (after all these years, Arizona finally won the lawsuit that said California was taking more than its share) is enough today—but won't be if people keep coming in at the rate of 1000 a day. You don't tell them anything. You keep pushing the plastic dream and pitching for more industry and more workers, and you look around for more water to con somebody out of.

That's Southern California today, and that was Southern California in the '40's and in the '50's. Northern Californians, the hustlers noted, had plenty of water. Look at the Feather River—3600 square miles of watershed, an annual average runoff of 4.5 million acre-feet (enough, for instance, to irrigate all the cotton in the state). But they would never give it to the hustlers down south. Northern Californians were wise to the con.

So the Southern California hustlers chafed, while the Big Guys —most of them northerners—waited with their arid, unproductive land while reaping millions from the land they had in production. But time was on their side.

By 1948 it was clear to the Big Guys that their plan to get the state to take over the Central Valley Project and then drop the 160-acre irrigation limitation had been blocked. And so, in hotel bars

and the spacious rooms of private clubs, the lords of the Valley talked with their counterparts in Southern California. They decided that together they could pull it off—with taxpayers' money, of course. You take some of the water, we'll take some. You have a majority of the voters down there and they can be conned into supporting the plan. All we have to do is invent an imminent water shortage and then dash in with a scheme for their salvation.

Then the Big Guys turned to something they've always been good at: word games.

There came into being, in 1950 or so, a group called the California Central Valley Flood Control Association (first word game). That group subsidized what looked like a routine flood control investigation by State Water Engineer A. D. Edmonston. His report, however, instead of being a routine report of a routine investigation, was something quite different. Its title (second word game) was *Report on Feasibility of Feather River Project and Sacramento-San Joaquin Delta Diversion Projects Proposed as Features of the California Water Plan.*

The California Water Plan had not yet come into being. But people were talking about *a* California Water Plan, in some circles anyway, and Edmonston and the people behind him wanted to be sure that their projects were in it.

The Feather River part was a fast shuffle. The important part of the plan, as far as its sponsors were concerned, was in the sneaky end of the title: *Sacramento-San Joaquin Delta Diversion Projects.* Water would be taken out of the Delta and sent south to irrigate the Big Guys' valuable lands, thus cutting the costs on the ones already being irrigated and bringing new lands into production.

The Feather River Project was a dam near the city of Oroville built to regulate the flow of that untamed river into an even and manageable year-round supply. The *reason* for the dam—useful as it proved to be, later, for flood control—had nothing to do with protection for the citizens of Yuba City and Marysville. The dam was constructed because without it the Federal Bureau of Reclamation might stick its nose into the Delta Diversion Project and say that the water being diverted was Central Valley Project water with its 160-acre limitation.

But the Feather River feeds into the Sacramento *below* the CVP projects in the north. By regulating its flow, the project planners could claim that the water being taken from the Delta is the controlled flow of the Feather (i.e., a *state* project) and that no limitations on its use could apply.

What's that you say? Water is water? Not in California.

Problem: At the Delta, the fresh water from the Central Valley meets the salt water of San Francisco Bay; the meeting place moves back and forth, sometimes well out toward the Bay, sometimes dangerously deep into the agricultural areas of the Delta itself. A part of CVP is the Delta Cross-Channel Canal, designed to take fresh Sacramento River water across the Delta without allowing it to mix with the Bay's salt water. But this water has the limitation on it.

Solution: Build another canal (the Peripheral Canal) around the Delta to the east. A pumping plant would lift the water and a new canal would take it down the west side of the San Joaquin Valley, virtually creating money as it flows.

It sounds simple. In principle, it is; but in practice it is something else. When Edmonston talked about moving water, he didn't fool around. The proposed Feather River Project (third word game: call the whole thing by that name) was by far the largest movement of water ever suggested. It has since engendered greater proposals (I have heard one for using Yukon River water in Mexico) but at the time it was, to use a once-familiar California word, colossal. The word about Edmonston's report got around, and pretty soon much of California, without quite understanding why, was talking about "the Feather River Project." No doubt the Big Guys, long master-users of publicity, had something to do with turning on the public to the exciting project, and seeing to it that the public saw it as an exciting project. Engineers loved it. Men in the street were impressed by it.

Northern Californians hated it.

The next four years brought a few engineering changes in the project, but the time was mostly spent in politics. Regularly the project was brought up in the legislature. Regularly northern senators or assemblymen would offer amendments. Regularly the

amendments would lose. Regularly the project would lose. What the northerners were trying to amend into the bill was, believe it or not, a homegrown, California copy of the 160-acre limitation on federal projects. It seemed as though a stalemate had been reached, which was hardly a satisfactory end to the struggle as far as the waterlords of the Valley were concerned.

When liberal "Pat" Brown ran for governor in 1958, backers urged him to endorse a 160-acre limitation for the Water Plan, but he refused; he *did* say he wouldn't stand for any "unjust enrichment" of big landowners. It was supposed to be the sort of liberal compromise which satisfies all parties. It satisfied practically nobody.

It was finally left to newly elected United States Senator Clair Engle to find a way around the 160-acre limitation: a two-price system. The waterlords would have to pay a little more for any water in excess of that necessary for the first 160 acres. But not too much more. Not enough to get in the way of the really massive profits that they would soon realize. And of course, they could have as much water as the size of their holdings made necessary. It was enough to swing a couple of votes in the deadlocked legislature.

The bare minimum cost of the Feather River Project would be, according to the most optimistic estimates of its optimistic partisans, about $2.5 billion. That was something like California's annual budget at the time, and nobody thought the California voters would pass a bond issue for two and a half billion dollars. So they trimmed it down to a figure which they thought the voters might buy, though it was still the largest state bond issue in the history of the United States: $1.75 billion. That's what went on the 1960 ballot as Proposition 1.

Opponents hooted. How, they wanted to know, can you build a $2.5 billion project for $1.75 billion? You can't. Quietly, the engineers cropped the project down to a smaller size, to be ready should the bond issue pass. As they were doing so, opponents of the project had no trouble finding economists to punch holes in the estimates. Inflation, they pointed out, would run the costs up too high. There would be problems selling the bonds. The $1.75 billion project, which was really a $2.5 billion project, would actually wind up costing closer to $4 billion.

They were right on all counts.

Labor (except for steelworkers, operating engineers and teamsters) opposed the bond issue. So did the Grange (historically, in California, the organization representing the "real" farmers). So did two independent consulting firms hired by the state to appraise the financing. So did 50 professors of economics from the state's leading universities. So even did two RAND Corporation scientists who published a paper on Southern California's water supply.

If San Diego had voted two-to-one for the project, it would have lost. San Diego, however, voted *four*-to-one for the project. Out of 5,842,712 voters, the difference was only 173,944 votes—but it was enough for passage. No Northern California county except the one in which Oroville Dam was to be built voted "yes."

The California Water Plan, then, is under way. (Final note on word games: For clarity we have used "Feather River Project" to describe what is properly that project *plus* the Delta diversion project. Today, however, that combination—the total of the project approved by the voters in 1960—has come to be called "The California Water Plan.") It has been under way for almost ten years. Oroville Dam exists, ugly but effective; you can drive up to an "overlook," view a display replete with superlatives that will tell you far more than you want to know about the dam and its construction, and look down on the dam itself. They had to move a whole railroad to build it. In the meantime, three other things have happened. Some Californians have learned a little more about the plan; some Californians have learned a little more about the costs; and some Californians have learned a little more about what I can only call—overworked word though it has suddenly become—ecology.

The current "official" estimate for the "final" cost of the California Water Plan is $2.75 billion. Whoever makes current "official" cost estimates knows perfectly well that this is hogwash—$4

billion is still closer to the truth. But if that admission were made, too many Californians might get mad. They want Californians to stay happy until this June, when they will be asked to vote "yes" on another ballot measure. It seems that California has this bunch of California Water Plan bonds from the 1960 issue, bonds they hung onto as long as possible—and now nobody will buy them. The state constitution says that you can't pay more than five per cent interest on state bonds (California has one of those constitutions that tell you everything except what color socks the governor may wear), and at five per cent, nobody will buy the damned things.

They have a fast $800 million worth of bonds still to be unloaded, and they figure that if they pay seven per cent, maybe somebody will buy them. If, I should say, Californians pay seven per cent. And whom will they pay? Mainly the Bank of America and its friends, who are the biggest moneylenders in the state, just as they are the biggest underwriters of the Big Guy "farmers."

So the costs of the California Water Project continue to escalate. Thanks to an ingenious free enterprise system, the people of California have the rare opportunity to pay for the privilege of watering the vast lands of the rich so that they can grow bigger cash crops and get even richer. But these costs are just the quantitative ones, merely the tip of the iceberg. To appreciate fully the bill which the people of California are going to pay for the honor of living in a society graced by institutions like the Bank of America, let us see what the California Water Plan will *really* do, if the voters let them finish it up this coming election.

First of all, it will—if it is extended to its planned limits, which are far beyond the currently authorized $3 billion or $4 billion project—destroy every natural river in California. There will be none without a dam, none without a man-made lake, none with natural fish and bird and invertebrate life. We don't know what all this will do to the ocean off Northern California; no one has ever asked. We don't know what it will do to the people whose living comes out of that ocean, or in a less important way to those who love to eat what others make their living catching.

Nor do we know what it will do to the climate of some lovely places, like the resort area of the Russian River, or to the Napa Valley, the heart of California's vineyards.

We know that canals and tunnels and dams and whatnot will be all over the place (the master plan calls for 370 more dams). It is already almost impossible to drive through, or to fly over, the Central Valley of California without seeing a canal, a pipeline or a gigantic row of metal towers carrying power lines. They are ugly. Agricultural land, artificial though the rows and crops may be, still somehow looks natural; it makes sense. A concrete canal does not look like a river.

We have talked about the enrichment of the few at the expense of the many. Along with this goes the continuing pollution of our information channels. Californians will be told again this spring that Proposition 7 is necessary so that Los Angeles can have its water (or, rather, they—the Southern Californians with the votes—will be told this). They will be told that again and again. The scare tactics will be dragged out as new appropriations, new authorizations are necessary. Our leaders, as much puppets on strings as any much-bemedalled Central American dictator, will lie to us. All right, they lie to us all the time; but I still don't like making it easy for them.

It is not only that the real purpose of the whole *megillah* has nothing to do with Los Angeles at all. Los Angeles might know that and still want their end of the culvert. It is that, in fact, Los Angeles does not need the water. The only sense in which Los Angeles (or San Diego, or Orange County or Riverside) can be said to *need* the water is in relation to projected figures of advertising-induced, immigrant population growth. When you provide services for this sort of a hustle, you make a decision: you have decided to support such growth; you have decided that you *want* it.

Thus, in Water Plan-opponent Alvin Duskin's phrase, Northern Californian water will go to Los Angeles in order to make more Los Angeles.

In the meantime, the Sacramento River keeps flowing, despite the existing CVP and the reduction of its flow by dam-building. At present, its fresh water outflow into the Delta is 18 million acre-feet a year. When the California Water Plan is finished, it will be two million acre-feet a year. So what?

So there is irrigation in the Sacramento Valley too, and the water dumps back into the river. It brings with it pesticide residues and minerals from the land; and in addition, the rivers in California, like those in New Jersey or Indiana, get a little industrial pollution. At the moment, in the Sacramento, all those things are diluted by 18 million acre-feet of water. Cut the flow to two million acre-feet, and you get a heavy gravy of pollutants.

In the Delta—one of the most beautiful and delicately balanced ecological systems this side of the Everglades, even as fouled up as it already is—this will make one hell of a lot of difference. If even one species of microscopic, brackish-water life disappears where the fresh water meets the salt water in the Delta, the ramifications, as I'm sure you know by now, can whiplash back through whole life chains, destroying dozens of species.

The land in the Delta—rich agricultural land—is in some places actually below the water level, and protected by levees. This is because of subsidence; if you fly over some of the islands in the Delta, you can see that they're saucer-shaped. The water underlies, as well as surrounds, the land—but it keeps it rich. Change that water and you can kill that land.

The pollutants in the water, of course, can't stop at the Delta, whatever their effect there. They would flow on out into San Francisco Bay. San Francisco Bay is an ecological mess, but there *are* all kinds of things still alive in it. We can kill the Bay if we want to; the California Water Plan may very well do so.

Okay. So much for the water that *isn't* transferred. What about the water that is?

You know that the Tigris-Euphrates Valley, now a desert, used to be a fruitful irrigated plain. There are areas like that in Pakistan, too, and elsewhere in the world. What happens is that the irrigation water first of all deposits various kinds of salts, thus making the soil more saline (or alkaline). At the same time, the irrigation process leaches some necessary minerals out of the soil, lowering its productivity.

There are ways of slowing up this process (they're very good at it in the Imperial Valley, at the southern end of California, which is a natural desert made to bloom just like in the poems), but in the long run you can't win. With present technology, at least, irrigation means, eventually, desert.

The trend is already clearly noticeable in the Central Valley, and particularly in the San Joaquin Valley, though of course destruction is not imminent. The San Joaquin River, as it used to flow before CVP made it virtually flow upstream, came into the Delta pretty heavily laden with these leached minerals, and it has left a lot of salts behind it. The only difference now is that it starts at the other end, and is then brought back to the Delta through an artificial channel. There was a move not long ago to use the channel for irrigation and to turn the actual San Joaquin River into a pipe. Modern man!

Now clearly, when this Sacramento River water is removed, by whatever means, across the Delta and into the San Joaquin Valley, it does not even have the advantage of being pure water to begin with. It's been used in the north. So it goes on being used, for irrigation, getting dirtier as it goes, not only with leached minerals but with pesticide residues and with anything else you can think of except maybe buffalo chips. But some of it is supposed to go to Los

VISTA POINT
SEE THE SAN JOAQUIN RIVER IN ALL ITS GLORY.

Angeles. Obviously, this now-filthy water can't be put back into the aqueduct and sent through the mountains to our southern neighbors. No, indeed: they get what *hasn't* been taken out for irrigation. What has been taken out is dumped into the San Joaquin drain and taken back to the Delta.

Or it was going to be, until we started to learn a little ecology. Now the Delta people and the Bay people have started to yell so loudly about this poisoned water—water which by the time it reaches the Delta may actually be "strong" enough to poison the land—that the planners have another idea, if you want to call it that.

They're going to divert it into Kesterson Reservoir, which I cannot locate precisely for you because it doesn't exist yet. The poisoned water, according to the current plan, will sit in Kesterson Reservoir until somebody figures out a way to clean it up or get rid of it.

Really. That's the "plan."

To love California is, alas, not necessarily to know it. There are millions of us who wander with delight among her mountains (did you know that Sequoia National Forest was originally created in order to drive out a succeeding socialist commune?), seek with joy her gentle valleys, enjoy her trees, her rolling hills, her awesome battle against the ocean—and who have no idea that she is a feudal state, held in thrall by a tiny few.

We need not kill ourselves through frenzied, irrational, needless growth; we need not labor to build stupid, destructive projects. But to achieve balance, we need first—of all things, in this most modern of states—a "land reform" which will make tortured, expensive and destructive schemes like the California Water Plan impossible.

Gene Marine is a free-lance journalist and author of The Rape of America *(Simon & Shuster). He is currently at work on a book titled* California!, *to be published by Atheneum in the fall.*

[Rural Renewal]

Trouble in Paradise

Sol Stern

> *"I went to the woods to live deliberately."*
> *—Thoreau,* Walden

When the military powers of California shot up and occupied the streets of Berkeley to destroy People's Park last May, it did so, according to Governor Reagan, to defend the inviolability of private property: If you want to "do your own thing," do it on your own land. Citizens of the little off-beat rural community of Canyon, just ten miles on the other side of the Berkeley hills, must have listened to this official rhetoric with a sense of irony. They do own their own land, yet this has not allowed them to do their own thing. Private property notwithstanding, in Canyon, just as in nearby Berkeley, the establishment has ruthlessly denied its own ethic of independence and individual initiative. Instead of sheriffs and shotguns, Canyonites face a limitless coercive bureaucracy. Instead of armed occupation, they face a new version of a familiar weapon—an onslaught of Rural Renewal.

Canyon isn't Drop City. It is a community, not a commune, a collection of artisans and professionals who care about their land and about its hundred-year history and traditions. Most of its residents are recent "drop-outs" in one way or another—if only from the sclerotic ugliness of the inner-city. But the energy and talents that they have withdrawn from the mainstream economy have been carefully re-invested in their own environment. Canyonites are like people all over the country who are leaving the boiling cauldron of the big city and seeking the space and freedom that is promised in the American dream. But they are finding that there is about as much trouble in their wooded paradise as there is in the urban hell.

[II]

Hidden away just beyond the reach of freeways and shopping centers, Canyon is about a 20-minute drive from the big cities of the Bay Area, up a steep hill going east, past $70,000 executive homes to an unmarked winding country road that dips suddenly into a rugged wilderness full of thick vegetation and topped by groves of redwood, oak and madrone trees. Three miles down this road there is a U.S. Post Office in a trailer, a little bridge with children playing around it and a pay telephone booth. A little further down is a two-room school modeled after the "little red schoolhouse" of the American past.

If you can't see any of the 45 homes that make up the community, it is because they are hidden in the thick forest up on the steep slopes of the canyon from which the community takes its name. Everything is still very much the way it looked over a hundred years ago when Canyon was not a retreat, but rather the economic center of the East Bay's thriving logging industry. Then, the lumberjacks lived in tents and cabins on the same wooded slopes where there are now handcrafted houses. There once were five brawling saloons doing business along the main road, and a stage coach joined the town with the sister city of Oakland. In its pioneer heyday, Canyon was a rough frontier town with its share of lynchings and shootings. The prime forest area was finally logged out, but for almost a century people have continued to seek out Canyon's isolation and rugged terrain, and to assume some of the hardy characteristics of the men who first built the town.

Because of its beauty and its inaccessibility to major highways, Canyon became one of the last enclaves to hold out against the swath cut by bulldozers and real estate schemes through once beautiful Contra Costa County, which is now a scramble of tract homes and ugly industrial towns. But as Canyon became more and more attractive, the powers that rule the adjacent municipalities discovered that it was an untapped mother-lode of potential subdivisions as well as a threat to the dominant suburban life-style.

In the name of progress the local water company became interested in the beautiful greenbelt area in which Canyon was centered. East Bay Municipal Utilities District (or East Bay MUD as it is generally known in the area) is legally a municipally owned utility which, under California law, ought to be controlled by the people in the district. But like most public utilities, it functions on a day-to-day basis as a monopoly responsible to no one but itself. It is notorious for the land speculation policies (promoted under the guise of protecting its watershed rights) which have made it one of the richest and largest landowners in California. An independent study made in the 1950's estimated that the company's excess lands were worth a potential $600 million in profits to any developer who subdivided them, built homes and sold them off—enough money to provide free water to every homeowner in the district for life. But the profits earned by East Bay MUD through its land speculations never result in lower rates for its customer-owners—only in increased wealth for the company.

In the early '50s, the water company turned its greedy eyes on Canyon and began to buy up all the available real estate in the area. To facilitate its land grabbing, East Bay MUD began a propaganda campaign claiming that Canyon's septic tanks were polluting the nearby creeks that ran into its reservoir—a charge which has never been substantiated by any independent investigation. In 1952 alone, the company bought up 24 Canyon houses and had them burned to the ground.

From 1950-1959, the population of Canyon dropped from 500 to 150, the number of homes from 110 to 40. At the little red schoolhouse, the number of children dwindled from 66 to 28. Many of the older residents became discouraged and gave up their homes without a struggle. But from the late '50s through the '60s, the direction of the migration reversed. A new breed of younger, hip pioneering types, fed up with life in the surrounding Bay Area cities, looked to Canyon, despite its problems, as providing the possibility of open space. To the local press and power structure, the new migration became a "hippie invasion." But while many of Canyon's men wear beards and long hair and the women long dresses and few bras, and while there is some pot around, the community is hardly an offshoot from the Haight-Ashbury. Indeed, there is a family solidity, a technical competence and a sense of privacy that gives Canyon the feel more of a California frontier town than of a hippie scene. Among the new Canyonites are an architect, an engineer, a contractor, and several auto mechanics, trained carpenters, social workers and teachers. Canyon people build their own homes, beautifully unorthodox but sturdy structures that blend in with the rugged terrain and greenery. They maintain and repair the community road and elect their own school board. They grow vegetables and fruit and raise chickens, goats and horses. And their children live in a paradise of tree houses, nature trails and animal life.

[III]

What is it like to live in Canyon? This is the way it was described by 26-year-old Sally Kehrer, who migrated from Berkeley three years ago: "... we are closely bound together by our love for the land and each other, by our mutual participation in the cycle of the seasons and by the overwhelming magic of this place called Canyon. Together we watch the flowers come with the warm days of spring—different flowers every week in the grass and among the trees. We watch the hills grow brown and dry in the summer. In the fall we gather to make wine by crushing the grapes and storing them in barrels. We come together in our houses in the cold windy rain of winter and talk in front of a fire. We help each other build what needs to be built—a house, a store, a porch, a septic tank.

"Each individual is loved and respected for himself, and the community is almost self-sufficient in individual skills. If you have something wrong with your car that you just can't seem to fix, you just call Malcolm or Tim. If you're planning to build anything and you need advice, ask Dave or George or Barry. If you have a problem with your water system, ask Doug or George or John....

"Once a month there's a community meeting where we talk about Canyon and its problems—or where we air our differences and discuss them together. Sometimes these meetings can be quite argumentative, but we usually leave feeling that something has been done and that we are all together again."

The president of the Canyon school board for the past eight years is 51-year-old George Menge, a tall, ramrod straight, pipe smoking father of seven daughters, who looks more like a small town Rotarian than one of the leaders of a "hippie" community. In fact Menge is a cop—a civilian criminal investigator for the U.S. Navy, a source of much good natured ribbing from his younger, stranger-looking friends in Canyon. "Yep, I guess I'm the fuzz," he chuckles when you ask him about it. Despite his occupation, Menge has been one of the toughest and most militant of the Canyonites in fighting back against the local establishment's attempts to intimidate the community. Nor has Menge's ostensible respectability protected him from the harassment meted out to Canyon's residents. Recently several of his dogs were picked up on his own property by the dog catcher, and the county building department has refused to give him a permit for a new barn.

Menge and his family live in a sprawling house (built mostly by Menge himself) in the midst of several acres of hilly Canyon land. His wife Virginia works part-time in the Canyon post office, and all of his daughters, ranging in age from 5 to 17, were educated in the little red schoolhouse down the road. "I started out here 23 years ago with just a small cabin, and then as my daughters came along, I kept adding new rooms and fixtures," says Menge. He also added horses, chickens, ducks, geese, pigeons and dogs. A familiar sight in Canyon is one of Menge's daughters, riding bareback up and down the canyon trails in a long, flowing dress.

In a warm, closely knit community like Canyon the "generation gap" is what it ought to be—a sense of mutual respect between young people and their elders, a dialectic of experience and spontaneity. Only in such a community could young "hippies" elect a 51-year-old cop to head their school board. For his part, George Menge says, "I let my kids run free. I let them associate with whomever they want. It's a good thing my kids and others don't live the way their parents do. If kids just did what their parents did, we never would have gotten out of the caves one million years ago. But I have a lot of hope for these kids. They're the ones who are really going to make the changes so the kinds of things that have happened to this community don't keep up."

Bob Trupin is a 37-year-old physicist and college teacher who moved out to Canyon with his wife Sue and their two children several years ago. Trupin had been active in Berkeley radical politics and Sue had participated in the Free Speech Movement at the

University of California in 1964; they now see the creation of small rural communities like Canyon as a valid part of the struggle to change society.

When East Bay MUD started pouring the heat on Canyon, Trupin wrote a letter to the local newspaper saying: "We in Canyon are the first line of defense in a fight which involves not only ourselves, but the people of the county—perhaps of the entire nation. For what is involved is the right of human beings to live in peace on their own land, in their own homes, in their own way. I know of no other community which has a deeper sense of responsibility to its residents, it neighbors, its ecology, to the future. And because of this responsibility we are determined not to be destroyed."

Tim Biggins' condemned house built without a permit. The County demanded that he put in two off-street parking spaces.

With the coming of families like the Trupins, the job of gobbling up Canyon became a little more difficult. The new settlers gave the community fresh hope and vitality. They were willing to fight for the land, and more importantly, they had the resources with which to wage the fight.

Recently a two-acre parcel of Canyon land came up for probate sale. The water company confidently made a bid of $16,000 to the court. The Trupins heard of the impending sale and practically overnight raised enough money from friends to outbid the company. A county courthouse full of natty lawyers and civil servants looked on in amazement as Trupin and other brightly-dressed Canyonites plunked down a certified check for $17,300 when the judge asked for the bids.

But it was 28-year-old Barry Smith, tall and bearded, with piercing blue eyes, one of Canyon's most creative builders, who organized the most spectacular defense against a water company land-grab. Smith heard that an 80-year-old widow named Mrs. Holmes was about to sell her 27 acres of choice Canyon land to the water company for $55,000, so he rushed to see her and talk her out of it. When he got to her house, he discovered that she had already signed a letter of intent to sell to the water company. Undaunted, Smith convinced her that Canyon would be destroyed if the water company got her land. He retained a high-priced real estate lawyer to get her out of her obligation to the water company and promised to raise $60,000 cash within several weeks to top East Bay MUD's bid. At the time Smith didn't have a penny, but within the allotted period, through word of mouth and ads in the underground press, he found 14 people who came up with several thousand dollars each to buy the land. This group of buyers decided that except for each individual's homesite, they would hold the land in common. They began to call themselves the Water Brothers Association, a name derived from Robert Heinlein's *Stranger in A Strange Land,* in which the sharing of water becomes the highest honor one man can bestow upon another—thus the notion of "water brothers."

[IV]

Stymied in its land maneuvers, the water company used its political muscle with the county government to make it impossible for the Canyonites to do anything with their land. Tim Biggins was denied a permit to rebuild his house, which had been destroyed by a fire, because his plans did not provide for "two off-street parking facilities." Biggins' house happened to be on the top of a rugged, steep slope; you couldn't get a mule up there, much less a motor vehicle. When George Menge asked for a permit to build a barn, he was told he didn't have enough land to house a secondary structure. So Menge arranged to lease an adjacent parcel. This time the inspector said that he couldn't put a secondary structure on a new parcel which had no primary structure.

Soon the local politicians too began to find it expedient to come down hard on Canyon. The local suburban newspapers began referring to Canyon as the "Haight-Ashbury" of Contra Costa County. John Nejedly, a politically ambitious D.A. (later elected to the state legislature), announced that Canyon was the source of the county's "drug problem." Big Jim Moriarty, chairman of the Board of Supervisors and a businessman with a hand in real estate, told a private community meeting that he had decided the "hippies" in Canyon had to go. The reason? He had become convinced the community was a menace when his wife came home from the shopping center one day and hysterically told him that she had seen some "dirty hippies" from Canyon handling the produce.

With the politicians joining the water company, Canyon began to feel the heat that local bureaucracies can generate when they work together. County narcotics officers, dog catchers, building inspectors and health officials became regular visitors. Several Canyonites were busted on trumped-up dope charges. Canyon people found that they couldn't cash checks at the nearest supermarket.

After the sale of the large tract of Canyon land to the Water Brothers, East Bay MUD convinced the Board of Supervisors to pass a new ordinance preventing the granting of septic tank permits within 1000 feet of any tributary to a reservoir. (Prior to this, the water company's official position had been that it required only a 300-foot *cordon sanitaire* around its watershed.) This ruling meant in effect that no new septic tanks could be built, and without septic tanks there could be no new building permits.

George Kehrer, one of the Water Brothers, recalls asking a county inspector just how he could live on his own land while he was

waiting for a permit to build a house. "Can I put up a tent?" asked Kehrer. "I'm afraid you can't," said the inspector. "How about putting in a camper?" asked Kehrer. "You can't do that either," said the inspector. "Well how about a sleeping bag?" said the exasperated Kehrer. Unable to find any reference to sleeping bags buried in his building code, the inspector said, "I guess that's O.K."

Some of the more adventuresome of the new Canyon residents went ahead and built on their land anyway. Traditionally the county solves building code hassles through a process of informal negotiations with the home owners, but in this case they staged a gestapo-style raid on the whole community. Canyon residents awoke one morning recently to find a small expeditionary force of twelve deputy sheriffs fully armed and helmeted, three narcotics agents, a dog catcher with a tranquilizer gun, and three building inspectors marching up and down their slopes, trespassing on their land and entering their homes, looking for "illegal structures" and other violations. When they had finished their mission, they had "posted" 20 structures (including a warehouse, a barn, a tree house for children, a chicken coop and a "sculpture"). Residents were told that anyone found in the houses after 48 hours would be subject to immediate arrest and that children would be taken off to juvenile hall. Canyon got a temporary injunction holding off any criminal action while it argued against the constitutionality of the building codes. But within several months the county had gone into phase two of its plan: it gave notice that if the posted houses were not dismantled within 45 days, the county would demolish the structures and bill the owners for the work. Although the deadline has passed and the matter is still in the courts, the people in the homes —and in a larger sense the entire community—continue to live under the axe.

One of the "illegal" structures is a beautiful geodesic dome built on a sturdy platform on the rim of the canyon. It is the home of Sally and George Kehrer, a young couple who were recently married at a ceremony in the local redwood grove. A local architect has said of the Kehrers' house, "If there were ever an earthquake in the area, I'd make book for their house to ride it out." Like most of the other posted homes, it is a unique architectural gem. Looking at the "Do Not Enter" sign that was posted on their dome, you reflect about the fact that in the eastern cnd of the county there are farm workers living in one-room dingy shacks which do not incur building code proceedings. And in the county's industrial city of Richmond, railroad workers are housed in box cars without any inspectors objecting. Looking over the canyon from his dome, George Kehrer recalls his emotions when the county's "authorities" found his house and posted it. "There was all this anger and helplessness, but we couldn't do anything about it. It was a nightmarish thing— something we had worked on so hard and all of a sudden there were these strangers there saying 'throw it all away.' "

To the Kehrers, both ex-Berkeley residents, the meaning of Canyon is in the living. "When we stand on our platform and look out over the hills and see smog everywhere except in Canyon, I know this is an alternative—I know I am breathing fresh air," says George. "In the last year living here I have learned more about animals, land, machinery, sewage, ecology and politics—everything that's important to my life and survival—than I could have learned in ten years in Berkeley."

[V]

Survival has become the name of the game in Canyon. In its struggle, the community came up with one last plan which took advantage of a provision in the State law allowing any unincorporated community to petition the county government for the creation of a "community services district for such purposes as sewage disposal and fire prevention services." A group of Canyon residents submitted such a plan to the Contra Costa Board of Supervisors.

The heart of their proposal was a unique and potentially revolutionary plan for sewage disposal drawn up by Doug McMillan, one of Canyon's resident experts. McMillan is a 37-year-old hydraulic engineer with a PhD from the University of California and a long list of impressive professional credentials. His sewage disposal plan called for the installation at every homesite of an individual, cheap and portable sewage treatment plant—aeration units just recently placed on the market. After initial treatment at each homesite, the water, now 95 per cent pure, would flow in pipes down to the bottom of the canyon to a pumping station from which it would be pumped up to a series of filters for further treatment. Finally the water, now 100 per cent pure and reusable for irrigation and as a fire-fighting reserve (which Canyon does not now have), would be collected in a tank at the top of the hill. The beauty of the proposed sewage system is its total application to the ecological and planning needs of Canyon.

The system, or variants of it, has obvious potential for other communities as well. It avoids the orthodox sewage disposal methods now being employed in the Bay Area which pipe untreated waste directly into the ocean—a process that has led to (among other ecological disasters) the pollution of the Bay and the destruction of a once flourishing fishing industry.

McMillan is a slightly built, quiet person who recently bought into the Water Brothers. He sat at his work-desk in his home (not posted) a while ago, and mused about his run-ins with the county bureaucracy. "When I first got out here I thought with my knowledge in the field I could talk reasonably to the county health people and work out the problems of the septic tanks. I saw my role as a protagonist for Canyon, so they couldn't fool us with their technical arguments. But I couldn't get anywhere with them. Finally Gerow [Ted Gerow, the county health department's sanitarian] told me that when it came to Canyon his mind was 90 per cent closed. When I pressed him on a specific technical point, like the question of pollution of the watershed, he would throw his hands up and say 'It's a matter of philosophy.' In the beginning I used to think these people at least were honest if misguided. Now I am more cynical about their motives."

A hearing on the proposed system was held a while ago in the neat, oak-paneled Supervisors' chambers. The entire county bureaucracy, plus all the experts the water company could dig up, had turned out to oppose the granting of the special district to Canyon. Their tactic was to deluge the Supervisors with technical objections to the proposed sewage system. Dr. McMillan's system was unfeasible, they argued. It had never been tested and there was no guarantee it would work. Besides, it was a complicated mechanical system and the people of Canyon could not be expected to maintain it themselves.

The county officials argued that instead of having its own system, Canyon should be incorporated into the county's central sanitation district (the same district that had recently been cited by State water officials for its pollution of the Bay). A sure-fire solution—except that it meant that Canyon's sewage (like the rest of the county's) would be dumped into the Bay and that it would cost each Canyon homeowner a prohibitive several thousand dollars extra to bring in central sewage. Most importantly for the future of the community, bringing in central sanitation (which would involve terracing the land, installing manholes about every 50 yards, etc.) would be the first step in opening up the whole region for real estate development and subdivision, thus threatening the greenbelt ecology of the area.

Bob Trupin sat in the spectator's gallery muttering at the insanity of it all. "They want to charge me $5,000 to dump my shit in the bay," he grimaced. Walking out of the hearing later, he turned around to look at the Supervisors, each of whom had been in office at least ten years; they were discussing a good citizenship award for some local Rotarian. He said in disgust, "They're a bunch of old men with no faith in the future and they haven't even made any provisions for the planet being habitable for more than another decade." If this were a rational society, its leaders, plagued with pollution, water shortages and the other problems strangling the planet, might see Canyon as an experimental ecology station. Canyon might be looked to as a living model of the frontier ethos that Ronald Reagan likes to talk about when he is on the stump. For it has the virtues of small government, self-help, community spirit, and respect for privacy and independence.

But rationality does not prevail, and our leaders are clearly engaging in empty rhetoric. On September 2, the Contra Costa Board of Supervisors voted 4 to 1 against allowing the residents of Canyon to have their own sewage district.

Canyon people aren't missionaries. But if there is anything that they would want people to learn from their community, it is that Americans must stop tearing up and exploiting the greatest gift bestowed on them, the *land*, and instead really start living on it. That would be their message to the outside world, but no one seems to be listening; and the freeways, the hot dog stands, the smog and the bulldozers keep creeping steadily closer to the rim of the canyon.

Sol Stern is a free-lance writer and frequent contributor to Ramparts.